freedom

WALKING
WITH GOD

living

HENSLEY
PUBLISHING

Walking With God from Slavery to Freedom
Learning to Live the Promise

ISBN 10: 1-56322-105-5
ISBN 13: 978-156322-1057

About Photocopying this Book

First Timothy 5:17-18 instructs us to give the laborer his wages, specifically those who labor in the Word and doctrine. Even so, some people who would never walk into a store and shoplift a book may think nothing of photocopying that very book. The results are the same.

Hensley Publishing has a moral, as well as a legal, responsibility to see that our authors receive fair compensation for their efforts. Many of them depend on the income from the sale of their books as their sole livelihood. So, for that matter, do the artists, printers, and numerous other people who work to make these Bible studies available to you. Please help us by discouraging those who would copy material in lieu of purchase.

DEDICATION

To my husband Mark

Thank you for loving me enough to allow me to take this journey
and for the encouragement and support along the way. I love you dearly.

And to Debbie Cleaver, Robin Lipe, Glenda May, and Tina Roeder

Thank you for your prayerful support and encouragement. You are beautiful,
godly women whose steadfast spirits challenge me to be a strong and courageous
servant of our Lord.

TABLE OF CONTENTS

week 1   DISCOVERING THE PROMISE   9

     day 1   A PROMISE INHERITED   10

     day 2   UNUSUAL PORTIONS   12

     day 3   AN UNLIKELY LEADER   15

     day 4   REHEARSING VICTORY   19

     day 5   PERSONAL APPLICATION   22

week 2   SHATTERED EXPECTATIONS   29

     day 1   BROKEN COMMANDMENTS   30

     day 2   GIANT-SIZED FEAR   33

     day 3   PROMISE DELAYED   37

     day 4   PASSING THE STAFF   40

     day 5   PERSONAL APPLICATION   43

week 3   A STEP OF FAITH   47

     day 1   A CALL TO LEADERSHIP   48

     day 2   A NEW SPIRIT   51

     day 3   THE CROSSING PLACE   55

     day 4   FAITHFUL MEMORIALS   58

     day 5   PERSONAL APPLICATION   62

week 4   THE BATTLES BEGIN   65

     day 1   FAITHFUL MARCH   66

     day 2   STUNNED BY DEFEAT   70

     day 3   THE WAGES OF SIN   73

     day 4   CITY OF PALMS   76

     day 5   PERSONAL APPLICATION   79

week 5   LESSONS FROM THE TRENCHES   85

     day 1   A SECOND CHANCE   86

     day 2   OUR FAITHFUL GOD   89

     day 3   THE GIBEONITE DECEPTION   93

     day 4   THE SUN STANDS STILL   97

     day 5   PERSONAL APPLICATION   100

week 6 DISCIPLINES OF ENGAGEMENT 105

    day 1   THE HABIT OF OBEDIENCE 106

    day 2   SIMPLE VICTORY 108

    day 3   REFLECTING VICTORY 111

    day 4   PRAISE HIM 115

    day 5   PERSONAL APPLICATION 118

week 7 SPIRITUAL BOOT CAMP 121

    day 1   THE BASICS 122

    day 2   A SACRIFICIAL VOW 128

    day 3   DECEPTIVE STRATEGIES 132

    day 4   THE ACCUSER 135

    day 5   THE EXERCISE OF PRAYER 138

week 8 PREPARED FOR VICTORY 143

    day 1   WEAPONS OF DEFENSE 144

    day 2   SHINY BOOTS 149

    day 3   HELMET OF SALVATION 152

    day 4   TAKING YOUR SWORD 155

    day 5   ADVANCED TRAINING 160

Week 9 THE PROMISED LAND 165

    day 1   A LESSER INHERITANCE 166

    day 2   THE LARGEST LOTS 169

    day 3   DWELLING PLACE REVEALED 172

    day 4   ALLOTTED PORTIONS 175

    day 5   PERSONAL APPLICATION 178

week 10 CLAIMING THE PROMISE 181

    day 1   A PLACE OF REFUGE 182

    day 2   FAITHFUL PROVISION 185

    day 3   RETURNING HOME 188

    day 4   MISSION ACCOMPLISHED 191

    day 5   PERSONAL APPLICATION 194

week 11 LIVING THE PROMISE 199

    day 1   ABRAHAM'S SEED 200

    day 2   THE SEAL 203

    day 3   FRUITFULNESS 207

    day 4   A FRUITFUL TASK 210

    day 5   THE PROMISED LAND 213

INTRODUCTION

Joshua was a man who walked with God. Through this study, you will witness his victories and his defeats, and you will discover what made the difference. If you're like me, you'll even see a little of yourself in Joshua. He was passionate, but at times presumptuous. He set his heart on obedience, yet sometimes he struggled to be "strong and courageous" as God commanded.

God promised Joshua and the Israelites an inheritance in the land of Canaan. But in order to receive that inheritance, they had to decide to leave Egypt behind and walk with Him into the land of promise. Sometimes they followed Him obediently and without question. Other times they chose their own way. Each decision impacted their journey.

As a believer in Christ, you are guaranteed an eternal Promised Land in heaven, but God has also given you a designated territory on earth where you can flourish as you use your gifts and talents for His glory along the way.

Joshua's journey represents ours as we walk with God through this life on our way to our eternal Promised Land. By following the progress of Joshua and the Israelites as they walked with God from slavery into freedom, you'll discover how their lives often paralleled the spiritual battles and struggles you encounter as you walk with God today.

In weeks seven and eight, you will take a two-week "leave" from the Israelite camp to attend Spiritual Boot Camp. It is my prayer that you will find this training to be a practical approach to the spiritual warfare you will encounter on your journey. You will study tangible, daily methods for putting on the "full armor of God" (Eph. 6:13), which will equip you to overcome the tactics of the enemy so that you can live the fruitful, victorious life God intends for you.

During the Spiritual Boot Camp segment of the study, you'll learn about your spiritual identity as a believer in Jesus Christ. Understanding your spiritual identity is vital if you want to walk in greater freedom through Christ.

Please fill out and redeem the coupon located on page 27. A spiritual identification tag, styled like a military id tag, will be sent to you in the mail at no extra charge to you. It is not a souvenir. The Spiritual Identification tag is a crucial element of the study. It will be a lasting reminder of your identity in Christ. Please take just a few minutes to complete the coupon and mail it in. If you are doing the study with a group, please coordinate with your group leader and mail the coupons in together.

It is my prayer that as you travel with Joshua from slavery in Egypt to freedom in the land of promise, you will find the courage to trust God more fully and walk with Him wherever He leads you in this life. May you also develop a greater yearning for the day when God fulfills His ultimate promise and you see your Savior face to face.

Walking with God is my greatest joy on this earth. I consider it a privilege to share this journey with you.

Mindy Ferguson

In order to better visualize their progress toward their Promised Land, on the map below, you'll plot the travels of Joshua and the Israelites. You'll need an inexpensive set of twelve colored pens or pencils to mark your map.

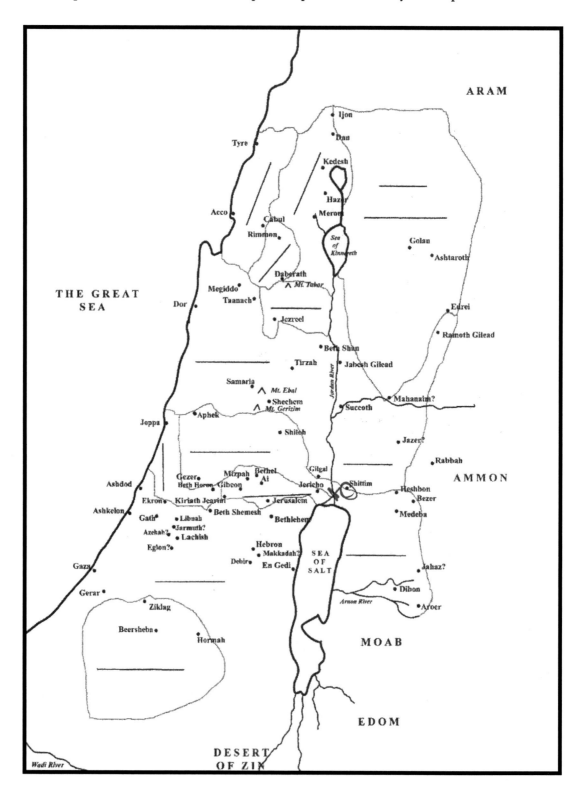

DISCOVERING THE PROMISE

My grace is sufficient for you, for my power is made perfect in weakness.

2 CORINTHIANS 12:9

week 1 • day 1

A PROMISE INHERITED

week 1 • day 2

UNUSUAL PORTIONS

week 1 • day 3

AN UNLIKELY LEADER

week 1 • day 4

REHEARSING VICTORY

week 1 • day 5

PERSONAL APPLICATION

week 1 · day 1

A Promise Inherited

I will establish my covenant as an everlasting covenant between me and you
and your descendants after you for the generations to come,
to be your God and the God of your descendants after you.
Genesis 17:7

The book of Joshua is a record of the Israelites' journey to claim the Promised Land. Today we will lay some groundwork for our study by identifying the specific land God promised to His people, and determining who the Israelites were and how they got their name.

Begin by reading **Genesis 17:1-8.**

What possession did God promise to give to Abraham's descendants (v. 8)?

The Land of Canaan

The land of Canaan was positioned between the Jordan River and the Mediterranean Sea, called "The Great Sea" at that time. Take a moment to look at your map on page 8. The land west of the Jordan River is the land God promised to Abraham and his descendants.

Now read **Genesis 17:15-19.**

God promised Abraham that he and Sarah would have a son through whom the covenant would pass to future generations. According to verse 19 what was the name of that son?

Isaac

Isaac had two sons of his own, named Esau and Jacob. God changed Jacob's name. What does **Genesis 35:10** tell us about Jacob's name?

No longer called Jacob
Israel

According to **Genesis 35:11-12**, what promise did God make to Jacob (Israel)?

Give land to descendants

Jacob (Israel) fathered twelve sons. Read **Genesis 29:31** through **30:24** and record their names. Note: You will only find eleven.

Reuben	*Joseph*
Simon	*Benjamin*
Levi	*Dan*
Judah	*Naphtali*
Issachar	*Gad*
Zebulun	*Asher*

Notice the last words of the passage: May the Lord add to me another son. God did just that. Read **Genesis 35:16-18** to find the name of the last son. Add it to the list above.

The old saying, "Be careful what you ask for" comes to mind! Can you recall a time when you prayed for something and the results were different than you expected? If so, record the circumstances.

_____

_____

_____

_____

According to **Genesis 49:28** what name was given to Jacob's descendants?

Israel

Scripture contains numerous references to the Twelve Tribes of Israel, also called the Israelites. On this journey, we will gain a wealth of personal insight as we read of the Israelites' struggles and triumphs. We will also discover that we serve a God who is faithful and who keeps His promises.

Write a prayer committing to complete this study. Ask God to strengthen your faith as you read His Word and do these lessons.

Father I don't want more Bible knowledge + another finished book. I want YOU! I want to know You + Hear You + Be more like You. CHANGE ME THROUGH THE power of Your Word.

UNUSUAL PORTIONS

I am your share and your inheritance among the Israelites.
Numbers 18:20

God promised the land of Canaan to Abraham and his descendants. Abraham's twelve great-grandsons (through his grandson Jacob) became the ancestors for whom the Tribes of Israel are named. When Canaan was divided into sections and each of the twelve tribes of Israel received their inheritance, the tribes of Joseph and Levi didn't inherit land in the same manner as the others. Today we will take a look at the unusual inheritance of these two tribes.

Let's begin with Joseph. What does **Genesis 37:3** tell us about his father's feelings for him?

_____

Most of us have heard the story of Joseph and his "coat of many colors" – a coat that must have been a constant reminder to his brothers of their father's favoritism. One day, Joseph bragged to his brothers about dreams he had that implied they would one day bow down to him (Genesis 37). Furious, Joseph's brothers plotted against him. They sold him to a caravan of Ishmaelites who took him to Egypt and sold him. To explain Joseph's disappearance, his brothers told their father that Joseph had been devoured by a ferocious animal.

In the course of time, Joseph came to the attention of Pharaoh, who realized that God was with Joseph. Pharaoh put Joseph in charge of the whole land of Egypt. He gave Joseph a wife, and Joseph fathered two sons.

Read **Genesis 41:50-52** and record the sons' names:

_____and_____

Years later, through a series of interesting events, Jacob and his remaining sons were reunited with Joseph and moved to Egypt. (Read Genesis 37-48.) When Jacob was very old, he became ill. Joseph, along with his sons, Manasseh and

Ephraim, went to visit Jacob.

Read **Genesis 48:1-20.** As Jacob was bestowing a blessing on his grandsons, he deliberately crossed his arms to place his right hand on Ephraim's head rather than on Manasseh's.

What was Jacob's response to Joseph's attempt to correct his father (**v. 19**)?

_____

Now read **Genesis 27:1-33.**

Joseph had probably heard the story many times of his father's obtaining Isaac's blessing by trickery. Perhaps when Joseph thought Jacob was mistaken as to which was the eldest son, he and Jacob both recalled the event. However, unlike Isaac, Jacob knew exactly what he was doing. He reassured Joseph that Manasseh would become great, but said that Ephraim would be greater.

Jacob adopted Ephraim and Manasseh as his own sons. In doing so, he gave Joseph's family a double share in the inheritance. So, Joseph's inheritance passed to his boys, and Ephraim and Manasseh became two of the tribes of Israel.

If you're keeping count, you noticed we now have thirteen tribes: (12 sons – Joseph = 11) + Ephraim + Manasseh = 13 tribes. However, the tribe of Levi, Jacob's third-born son, also received an unusual portion, a special gift.

Read **Numbers 18:20-24.**

God Himself was the Levites' inheritance. They did not receive land that they could call their own. Instead, they became responsible for the care of the sanctuary and the altar.

Now read **Numbers 35:1-3.**

How did the Lord provide for the Levites?

_____

_____

_____

Let's update our formula:

(12 sons – Joseph = 11) + Ephraim + Manasseh - Levi = 12 tribes

Look back at the list of the twelve tribes that you made on page 11. Now list the tribes, substituting and deleting as described above.

_____   _____

_____   _____

_____   _____

_____   _____

_____   _____

_____   _____

These are the twelve tribes of Israel that inherited the land of Canaan. We will refer to them often. Tomorrow we will continue our background. We will begin by studying the Israelites' journey prior to Joshua's call to leadership.

week 1 · day 3

An Unlikely Leader

My grace is sufficient for you, for my power is made perfect in weakness.
2 Corinthians 12:9

In the next few lessons, we'll study the life of Moses. He preceded Joshua as the Israelites' leader and led the people to the border of the Promised Land. Moses was Joshua's leader, teacher, and mentor. As we briefly study Moses' life, you will see that Joshua couldn't have had a better mentor.

Begin by reading **Exodus 2:1-25.**

The Hebrew word translated as "remembered" in verse 24 is *zaka*. It means "to mark, so as to be recognized, to make mention of, to recount, to be mindful of."

Write **Exodus 2:24.** Replace the word remembered with "was mindful of."

_____

_____

_____

_____

_____

God didn't forget His covenant and then suddenly remember it when the Israelite slaves cried for help. God was mindful of it as He heard their desperate cries. He knew every hurt and saw every tear. From the day they became enslaved, God had a plan for the Israelites' deliverance. Even before Moses was born, God knew he would be their deliverer.

By command of Pharaoh, Moses should have been killed at birth. Instead, he was strategically moved into the position of grandson to Pharaoh himself. God had a plan for Moses, and He revealed it at the proper time.

Years after Moses had fled Egypt, he was shepherding for his father-in-law when he caught sight of a bush that was on fire. Strangely, the bush didn't burn up. When Moses went over to inspect this strange phenomenon, the Lord spoke to him.

Read **Exodus 3:7-11**.

What was Moses' response to God (v. 11)?

_____

Moses doubted his ability to lead. He focused on his unworthiness and lack of authority, just as we often do. But if God says He is sending you, He will equip you to accomplish the task. And it is when we feel the most inadequate and unqualified that we are best able to humbly serve God, wholeheartedly submitting to His will.

Despite Moses' doubts, God was patient with him. In the beginning, God strengthened Moses' faith by acting through Aaron, but as Moses followed instructions and negotiated with Pharaoh, God molded him into a leader.

As God brought ten plagues on Egypt in a campaign to cause Pharaoh to free His people, He was nudging Moses into his leadership role. Let's skim the accounts of the first few plagues and record the way God did it.

PLAGUE	WHO ACTED
1. Blood (**Exodus 7:14-21**)	_____
2. Frogs (**Exodus 8:5-6**)	_____
3. Gnats (**Exodus 8:16-17**)	_____
4. Flies (**Exodus 8:20-24**)	God

(Notice this time Moses spoke and God acted. Aaron took a backseat.)

5. Livestock (**Exodus 9:1-5**)	_____
6. Boils (**Exodus 9:8-10**)	_____
7. Hail (**Exodus 9:13-24**)	_____

Moses took the lead from this point on. God allowed Aaron to act until Moses' faith was strong enough to carry out God's instructions on his own.

Now read **Exodus 12:31-36**.

God freed His people through Moses. The gentle patience of God allowed Moses to grow into the leader he needed to be.

If we are willing, God patiently molds us into the vessels He needs to accomplish His purposes. Are you doing anything now that you wouldn't have believed possible a year ago? If so, describe the circumstances.

_____

_____

_____

_____

Read **Exodus 14:5-16, 21-28**.

In their flight from Egypt, the Israelites became trapped between Pharaoh's army and the sea. God patiently instructed Moses, "Raise your staff and stretch your hand over the sea." When Moses responded with faith, God parted the water.

Some of our trials and struggles seem just as terrifying and impossible to overcome as the Israelites' predicament at the banks of the Red Sea. How often we fail to act! We look at the obstacles instead of looking to the God who can take us through them.

As Moses took action, he gained courage and confidence in the Lord. But he acquired something else that was crucial to his success as a leader. Read **Exodus 14:31** below.

> *When the Israelites saw the great power the Lord displayed against the Egyptians, the people feared the Lord and put their **trust** in him and in Moses his servant.* (emphasis added)

Moses gained the people's trust. People will only follow a leader they trust and respect. Moses gained the courage and confidence he needed by walking closely with God and obeying His instructions. Because Moses first followed God, the Israelites were willing to follow him.

God gave Moses the grace to overcome his weaknesses and accomplish what he could never have done on his own. Truly God's grace is sufficient!

> *My grace is sufficient for you,*
> *for my power is made perfect in weakness.*
> 2 Corinthians 12:9

What is your "Red Sea" at this time?

_____

_____

_____

_____

_____

_____

_____

_____

Take a moment to thank God for His sufficient grace.

week 1 · day 4

REHEARSING VICTORY

*The Lord said unto Moses, "Write this for a memorial in a book,
and rehearse it in the ears of Joshua."*
Exodus 17:14 KJV

Yesterday, we saw Moses struggle to accept his role as leader. As we observe his leadership in action today, we will get our very first glimpse of Joshua.

We left off at the banks of the Red Sea, where God allowed the Israelites to cross on dry ground. The Egyptians, attempting to pursue them, were destroyed as the waters of the sea returned and covered them. In celebration, Moses and the men sang a song of praise to God and the women danced with tambourines.

Read **Exodus 15:19-21**.

It is important to celebrate our victories. We often move from one task to the next, never stopping to celebrate and thank God for our success.

Have you ever danced before the Lord in celebration? Take a moment to record some of the many ways God has provided for you and brought victory to your life. Put on some God-honoring music and "cut a rug" before your Lord!

_____

_____

_____

_____

The Israelites enjoyed a wonderful celebration of victory. But their joyous dispositions didn't last for long. Read **Exodus 15:22-25** and **16:1-15**.

The Lord provided for His people. He gave them water to drink and manna from heaven to eat. Little did the Israelites know that they would continue to depend on God's provision every day for forty years just to survive.

The Israelites traveled from place to place until they camped in Rephidim, where they were attacked by a group of nomadic desert people called the Amalekites.[1] It is during this battle that we are introduced to Joshua.

Read **Exodus 17:8-16**, then read the KING JAMES VERSION of verse 14 below:

> *The Lord said unto Moses, "Write this for a memorial in a book, and*
> *rehearse it in the ears of Joshua."* (emphasis added)

From the very first mention of Joshua in Scripture, God was training him for his eventual role as leader. The Lord wanted to make sure he was fully aware that it was God Himself who won the battle for the Israelites.

Today we erect many memorials to remember heroes or events of great significance. When Moses raised his hands to the Lord, he acknowledged God as the victor, honoring Him with all the glory.

There would be many battles in Joshua's future. God wanted to make sure Joshua didn't trust in his own ability, so He told Moses to "rehearse it in the ears of Joshua."

One definition of *rehearse* is "to practice for a performance."[2] Moses was to rehearse the event over and over so that Joshua would know what to do when it was his time to "perform."

God produces many rehearsals in our lives. He can use each of our experiences, good or bad, to prepare us for what lies ahead. If we trust God and submit to Him in every circumstance, we will come through the situations wiser and stronger. These rehearsals give us the faith and courage we need to accomplish the tasks God intends for us.

Can you think of a situation, good or bad, that God used to make you stronger or prepare you for a task He called you to do later? If so, explain.

_____

_____

_____

_____

Scripture doesn't document events just for history's sake. Every account has a purpose and a lesson. Let's discover another of Joshua's lessons.

Read **Exodus 24:12-18.**

Notice the wording in verses 13-14 below.

*Then Moses set out with **Joshua** his aide, and Moses went up on the mountain of God. He said to the elders, "Wait here for **us** until we come back to you." (emphasis added)*

Who was on the mountain with Moses? _____.

Now read **Exodus 25:1-9** and **31:18**.

During those forty days and forty nights, God gave Moses both the Ten Commandments written on tablets of stone, and the pattern for the tabernacle, the sanctuary where God's people would worship and speak to Him.

Imagine the emotions Moses felt as he started down that mountain. He'd spent forty days in the presence of God Almighty Himself. He was being appointed General Contractor, so to speak, in the construction of God's sacred tabernacle.

What does **Hebrews 8:5** tell us about this sanctuary?

_____
_____
_____
_____

Moses must have been in awe of all he had been commissioned to accomplish. And Joshua? He must have anxiously awaited Moses' recount of the forty-day visit with God. He probably rehearsed a few of God's words in his heart, himself, on the hike down.

PERSONAL APPLICATION

day one

God promised to make Abraham the father of many nations, to be his God and the God of his descendants. In addition, God promised to give his descendants the land of Canaan as an "everlasting possession."

As we identified the twelve tribes of Israel, what did you find most interesting?

_____

_____

_____

_____

According to **Numbers 18:21**, what did God give the Levites in return for the work they did while serving at the Tent of Meeting?

_____

One tenth of all that was in Israel was to support the Levites. Giving a tithe was not a suggestion; it was an obligation and was not negotiable.

Read **2 Corinthians 9:7**.

Because everything we own is by God's grace, whether we give ten percent or fifty percent, we are only giving back a portion of what He has given us. So, we shouldn't give out of necessity or legal pressure; we should give with a grateful and cheerful heart. And how much should we give? God believed the Levites deserved ten percent. But whatever we give, it should be proportional to God's blessing. One tenth of our income should be the minimum.

Spend a few moments in prayer about your giving. Ask God to show you any adjustments you might need to make.

day two

The tribes of Joseph and Levi each received unusual inheritances compared with the other tribes.

How do you think the other tribes reacted to Joseph's double portion? What about the fact that the Levites would live off of the Israelites' tithes and be given land within the territories of the other tribes?

_____

_____

_____

_____

How do you react when you see others receiving what you perceive to be more than their fair share of money or rewards? What about when others are given part of your territory in ministry or at work?

_____

_____

_____

_____

The Levites were responsible for teaching the Israelites God's law. Had they all been located in one territory within Canaan, God's people would have lacked exposure to godly instruction and counsel. God's provision ensured that everyone would have access to training from the priests.

We don't always understand it, but God has a purpose for all He does. At times when we think we have been overlooked or slighted, we need to admit those feelings to God and then trust Him. Sometimes that is difficult, but when God makes us share territory or withholds His blessings, it is always for the greater good.

day three

When God told Moses to bring His people out of Egypt, Moses responded with fear and doubt. Let's take a look at his initial responses to God.

Read **Exodus 4:8-13**.

Is God calling you to a task that you feel inadequate or unprepared to accomplish? If so, explain:

_____

_____

_____

_____

God required Moses to act as he stood on the shore of the Red Sea. What did Moses' action reveal to God?

_____

According to **Hebrews 11:6**, what is required to please God?

_____

Moses wasn't eloquent. He was a "man slow of speech and tongue" (**Exodus 4:10**), and he was full of self-doubt. Yet God accomplished great things through him.

God often chooses unlikely vessels to carry out His work. It is when we feel the least qualified that we are most usable. God can do more with our humble efforts than with all the credentials in the world. He doesn't want us to trust in our experience or education. He wants us to trust in Him and Him alone. For it is then He receives the greatest glory.

Read the words that were written of Moses after his death (**Deuteronomy 34:10-12**).

God can perform awesome deeds through us just as He did through Moses. But we must have enough faith to be usable vessels.

day four

Reread **Exodus 17:14**.

God told Moses to record the battle with the Amalekites and to make sure that Joshua heard it. It was important to God that Joshua would never forget whose power won the battle.

Has there ever been an incident in your life that God led you to memorialize? If so, what was it and how did you remember the event?

_____

_____

_____

_____

Read 2 Corinthians 3:1-3.

God is preparing you for future tasks or positions just as He prepared Joshua. In fact, you already have a crucial role in the body of Christ. Christians are ministers of the new covenant.

Another word for *minister* is *ambassador*, an authorized representative or messenger. Through Christ, you are an authorized messenger of the Gospel, the new covenant. Evidence of this covenant is written not on tablets of stone, but on human hearts.

The best "letters of recommendation" in ministry are the lives of the people impacted. Is there a ministry that has affected you to the extent that your life would be a letter of recommendation? If so, describe that ministry.

_____

_____

_____

_____

> *Not that we are competent in ourselves to claim anything for ourselves,*
> *but our competence comes from God.*
> *He has made us competent as ministers of a new covenant.*
> 2 Corinthians 3:5-6

Ask God to impact others through you to the point that their lives become letters from Christ, written on the tablets of their hearts.

SPIRITUAL IDENTIFICATION TAG COUPON

During the Spiritual Boot Camp segment of the study (Weeks 7 and 8), you'll learn about your spiritual identity as a believer in Jesus. Understanding your spiritual identity is vital if you want to walk in greater freedom through Christ.

Please fill out and redeem this coupon by folding the page in half, sealing it with a small piece of tape, stamping it, and mailing it to the publisher. A Spiritual Identification tag, styled like a military id tag, will be sent to your US address at no extra charge. It is not a souvenir. The Spiritual Identification tag is a crucial element of this study. It will be a lasting reminder of your identity in Christ.

Please take just a few minutes to complete the coupon and mail it in. If you are doing the study with a group, please coordinate with your group leader and mail the coupons in together.

fold here

Name _____

Address _____

_____

City _____ State _____ Zip _____

Telephone _____

Email Address _____

If you are participating in a group study, please give us the name of church or group where you are attending, and the leader's name.

Church You Attend _____

Group Leader _____

Name _____

Address _____

City _____

State _____ Zip _____

WWG

HENSLEY PUBLISHING

6116 E 32ND ST

TULSA, OK 74135-5494

SHATTERED EXPECTATIONS

The Lord himself goes before you and will be with you;
he will never leave you nor forsake you.
Do not be afraid; do not be discouraged.

DEUTERONOMY 31:8

week 2 • day 1

BROKEN COMMANDMENTS

week 2 • day 2

GIANT-SIZED FEAR

week 2 • day 3

PROMISE DELAYED

week 2 • day 4

PASSING THE STAFF

week 2 • day 5

PERSONAL APPLICATION

BROKEN COMMANDMENTS

When Moses approached the camp and saw the calf and the dancing,
his anger burned and he threw the tablets out of his hands,
breaking them to pieces at the foot of the mountain.
Exodus 32:19

We left Joshua and Moses descending Sinai after Moses spent forty days and forty nights at the top of the mountain with God. They probably marveled at God's plans for the Tabernacle. Perhaps they trembled at the detailed commands God expected His people to obey. They might have studied the tablets of stone, awestruck by the fact that they were inscribed by God Almighty Himself. But all was not well in the Israelite camp. The people had grown restless during their leader's absence.

Read **Exodus 32:1-24.**

Moses and Joshua probably felt just as broken as the shattered tablets lying at the foot of the mountain. Moses had been gone only forty days and already the people were worshiping a golden calf. Ironically, that calf had been made from the very jewelry the Israelites had received from the one true God as plunder from the Egyptians.

Undoubtedly Moses was crushed by the Israelites' betrayal, just as parents are wounded when one of their children chooses to behave contrary to his or her upbringing.

Read **Exodus 32:31-34.**

Moses was a dedicated leader. The character he displayed when dealing with the people's sin is inspiring. What request does verse 32 tell us Moses made of the Lord?

_____

Moses was deeply devoted to the Israelites' wellbeing. He asked God to blot him out of His book if the people's sin could not be forgiven.

To learn what "book" Moses was talking about, read **Revelation 3:5**.

Moses felt such responsibility for the people's actions that he thought God should "blot out" his name from the Book of Life.

This is the first mention in Scripture of this book. God must have shared the meaning of the book with Moses. Having his name removed would result in eternal separation from God. We don't know if Moses fully understood the consequences of such a request, but he took his leadership responsibility seriously. He led with inspiring devotion and character.

Joshua watched these events unfold. He witnessed Moses' devotion to God's people. What a privilege to be the aide to a man of such integrity. Let's take a look at another great privilege Joshua experienced in preparation for leadership.

Read **Exodus 33:7-11**.

This "Tent of Meeting" was not the actual tabernacle that was to be constructed according to the pattern God gave Moses. In Moses' excitement and anticipation, he would "take a tent and pitch it outside the camp some distance away." What a passionate man Moses was! He so longed for that dwelling place where the glory of the Lord would rest that he set up a representation – a symbol for it. God honored his enthusiasm by meeting with him in this tent and speaking to him "as a man speaks with his friend."

What does verse 11 tell us about Joshua?

We don't know what Joshua did in the tent, but we do know he had first-hand knowledge of Moses' relationship with God. Let's skip ahead and see why this might be of particular importance to Joshua later on his journey.

Read God's words to Joshua.

As I was with Moses, so I will be with you; I will never leave you nor forsake you.

Joshua 1:5

Joshua needed to understand the relationship between Moses and the Lord. God placed Joshua in the position of Moses' aide to strengthen and prepare him. That assignment was as much for Joshua's benefit as for Moses'.

Is there someone in your life whose relationship with God inspires you? If so, what have you witnessed that you would like to cultivate in your relationship with the Lord?

_____

_____

_____

_____

_____

_____

_____

_____

This is the last time Joshua is mentioned in the book of Exodus. The remainder of Exodus, for the most part, gives details for the construction of God's glorious tabernacle.

week 2 • day 2

GIANT-SIZED FEAR

We saw the Nephilim there (the descendants of Anak come from Nephilim).
We seemed like grasshoppers in our own eyes, and we looked the same to them.
Numbers 13:33

The Tent of Meeting, or tabernacle, was completed and Moses set up the courtyard around it as the Lord commanded. Moses "finished the work" and the "glory of the Lord filled the tabernacle" (**Exodus 40:33-34**).

Read **Exodus 40:36-38.**

The Israelites always knew exactly how long the Lord intended for them to remain in a certain location. How did they know?

_____

_____

_____

Don't you wish God would place a pillar of cloud over the places you are to "camp" and lift it when it is time to move on?

Is there a task or place where you are "camped" right now that you sense God may want you to move from? If so, what is it?

_____

_____

_____

Ask God to be as clear with you as He was with the Israelites.

The Israelites traveled from place to place until they came to the Desert of Paran. From there, Moses sent spies to scout out the Promised Land of Canaan – the land flowing with milk and honey. One of those men was Joshua.

Read **Numbers 13:1-3, 16.**

What was Joshua's birth name? (v.16) _____.

Pronounced "ho-shay-ah," the name *Hoshea* means "deliverer." Moses changed Hoshea to Joshua. The Hebrew is *Yehowshuwa*, which means, "The Lord saved."

Look back at the lesson from Week One, Day Four. Can you think of any reason Moses might have changed Hoshea's name?

_____

_____

God wanted Moses to make absolutely certain Joshua understood that it was God's power, not Joshua's, that had saved the Israelites from the Amalekites. God must have instructed Moses to change Hoshea's name to Joshua so he would have a constant memorial of his dependence upon God.

Do you find it interesting that Joshua held names meaning both "deliverer" and "the Lord saves"? Just as the place Moses called the Tent of Meeting was a symbol of the actual tabernacle to come, Joshua was a symbol for Christ – the true Deliverer and Savior. As a matter of fact, "Jesus" is the Greek translation of the name Joshua.

Read **Numbers 13:25-33.**

After forty days the scouts returned from exploring the land. What did the other scouts say they looked like compared to the people in Canaan?

_____

In the KING JAMES VERSION, verse 33 refers to these men of great size as giants. This was certainly not a good report. Caleb had seen the same things as the other men, yet he had faith that they could "go up and take possession of the land."

Unfortunately, the people didn't seem to be able to get those giants out of their minds, and as a result they were afraid. Read **Numbers 14:1-11.**

Fear is the most crippling and defeating of all human emotions. At times, it can even rob us of the ability to move. Fear is the complete opposite of faith. As we saw through the plagues on the Egyptians, God required Moses to act in faith before releasing His power.

God hath not given us the spirit of fear; but of power,
and of love, and of a sound mind.
2 Timothy 1:7 KJV

The word *fear* in this verse comes from a Greek word that implies one is faithless. Scripture tells us "without faith, it is impossible to please God" (**Hebrews 11:6**). It is impossible to please God when we allow fear to control us. Fear is proof of lack of faith.

Caleb and Joshua tore their clothes as an expression of grief. They pled with the Israelites not to be afraid and "rebel against the Lord." They knew the fear and disbelief of the Israelites was rebellion against God and would bring dire consequences.

In **Numbers 14:11**, we see God asking, "How long will they refuse to believe in me?" Notice He didn't say, "How long will they refuse to believe me?" He said "believe in me." There is a significant difference.

Read **John 1:1**:

In the beginning was the Word, and the Word was with God,
and the Word was God.

We cannot separate God from His Word.

Read **Deuteronomy 7:17-19**. What had God said He would do for the Israelites?

_____

_____

God said He would drive out the current inhabitants of the Promised Land. That included those giants. Yet despite the pleading of Caleb and Joshua, the Israelites stood at the border of their Promised Land, and allowed fear to paralyze them. They refused to believe they could take the land God had promised them. They refused to believe God was greater than the giants. Their disbelief of God's Word was, in effect, disbelief in God Himself.

At times in our walk with God, He calls us to do things that can only be accomplished with His power. Have you ever allowed "giants" to keep you from believing in God's ability to accomplish His work through you?

_____

_____

_____

_____

As a way of closing, spend the rest of today asking God to reveal the "giants" in your life.

week 2 · day 3

PROMISE DELAYED

Not one of you will enter the land I swore with uplifted hand to make your home,
except Caleb son of Jephunneh and Joshua son of Nun.
Numbers 14:30

We last left the Israelites at the border of the Promised Land. Ten of the spies had given a bad report about giants and the people cowered. Joshua and Caleb begged the people to trust God, but the people refused. That decision cost them dearly.

Read **Numbers 14:10-34** and answer the following questions.

As a result of their fear, how many years would the Israelites wander in the desert?

_____

Why did God choose this particular number (**v. 34**)?

_____

According to **verse 30,** what men would actually enter the Promised Land?

_____

Never underestimate the consequences of rebellion. When the Israelites' fear led to open rebellion, they even threatened to stone Moses, Caleb, and Joshua and "choose a new leader" (**Numbers 14:4**). Yet Moses chose to intercede on their behalf, despite their disrespect and grumbling against him. He fell on his face and prayed earnestly for them.

If you were in Moses' shoes, how do you think you would have reacted to the Israelites' hostility toward you as their leader?

_____
_____
_____
_____

Most of us would struggle to forgive the people, let alone pray that God would relent and pardon them. Aren't you struck by the loyalty of Moses?

Scripture tells us that as believers in Christ, we also have powerful intercessors praying for us. According to **Romans 8:26-27, 34**, who intercedes for us?

_____ and _____

Have you ever thought about the fact that the Holy Spirit and Jesus Christ actually intercede on your behalf? Nothing you can do could ever separate you from the love of Christ. He sits at the right hand of the Father, always interceding for you. Doesn't it comfort you to know who you have praying for you in times of crises?

Take a few moments to thank God for your powerful intercessors.

God granted Moses' requests. He forgave the Israelites and spared their lives. But although God forgave the Israelites, the consequences of their sin remained. Because of the way the Israelites had handled their fear, the joy of reaching the Promised Land was stripped away from an entire generation of God's people. Of all the men over twenty years old, only Caleb and Joshua were allowed to enter the Promised Land.

Has there ever been a time when, although your sin was forgiven, you had to live with consequences long afterward? If so, what did you learn from enduring the consequences of your actions?

_____

_____

_____

_____

_____

_____

_____

_____

_____

_____

We would fall right back into the same sin patterns if we never experienced any consequences. As with the nation of Israel, God uses consequences to kill off rebellion.

Sadly, at the very border of the Promised Land the Israelites were told to "turn back." Faced with such rebellion, God delayed fulfilling His promise until the next generation became adults.

week 2 · day 4

PASSING THE STAFF

The Lord himself goes before you and will be with you;
he will never leave you nor forsake you.
Do not be afraid; do not be discouraged.
Deuteronomy 31:8

The Israelites had been sentenced to forty years in the wilderness. During that time, the men who had been enslaved by the Egyptians died and a new generation grew up. This group of Israelites had never experienced slavery; they had learned to depend totally upon God for survival, day after day.

Today, we will pick up as the Israelites approached the Promised Land for the second time. We will see the transition of leadership from Moses to Joshua. We will also witness the death of Moses – a man to whom God spoke as a man speaks with his friend (**Exodus 33:11**).

But first, let's read about the incident that banished Moses from the Promised Land. Read **Numbers 20:1-13**.

Moses had freed the Israelites from slavery and built the tabernacle. He spoke to God as a friend, and led God's people faithfully for forty years. Yet his lifelong dream of entering the Promised Land was shattered.

At the waters of Meribah, Moses became resentful toward God's people. He spoke harshly, acting as though he and Aaron were the ones providing the water for them. After all those years of faithful service, Moses blew it. He lashed out at God's people and didn't trust God to handle their rebellion. By striking the rock rather than speaking to it, Moses not only drew attention to himself, robbing God of the glory, he also struck what was intended to be a symbol of Christ and His provision.

What was the reason God gave for not allowing Moses to bring the Israelites into the Promised Land (v.12)?

_____

_____

_____

Stealing God's glory is a serious issue.

What does **Isaiah 42:8** tell us?

_____

_____

Moses failed to honor God as holy in the sight of the Israelites. He robbed God of the glory for His provision. He struck the rock. As a result, Moses was denied the privilege of entering the Promised Land.

Now read **Numbers 27:12-17**.

Moses had lost his own dream, but he was still concerned for the Israelites' wellbeing. He requested that God appoint a man to "lead them out and bring them in" – a shepherd for the flock.

God appointed Joshua to be that shepherd.

From what we've read about the Israelites, why do you think Moses thought they would need a shepherd after he was gone?

_____

_____

_____

_____

Read **Numbers 27:18-23**.

What did God tell Moses to do so that the Israelites would obey him (**v. 20**)?

_____

Let's see how Moses responded. Read **Deuteronomy 31:1-8**.

Moses passed his authority to Joshua by declaring, in the presence of all Israel, that the Lord would go before Joshua and be with him.

The Israelites had experience with Moses and they trusted him when he, in effect, passed the staff of God to Joshua. Joshua took his assignment knowing the incredible burden Moses had carried throughout their time together.

Have you ever witnessed anyone in a leadership position carrying a heavy burden? If so, what have you learned from watching their example?

_____

_____

_____

_____

Take this opportunity to write notes of encouragement to the person(s) in your example above. You just may lighten their load a bit.

week 2 · day 5

PERSONAL APPLICATION

day one

When Moses and Joshua came down Mount Sinai and saw the people dancing and worshiping the golden calf, Moses was so angry that he threw the Ten Commandments on the ground.

According to **Exodus 20:3-4,** what were the first two commandments on the tablets?

_____

_____

_____

_____

The Israelites couldn't even handle the first two commandments, let alone all ten. Moses' thoughts must have returned to those first few words on the tablets as he was confronted with this scene. The broken tablets were a fitting representation of the entire situation.

The people wanted a God they could touch and see – something tangible to place their trust in. How sad it is that Aaron fashioned an idol out of the gold that God so graciously provided as they exited Egypt. Unfortunately, we often do the same thing. We place our trust in God's provision rather than in Him as our provider.

What golden calves have you placed your trust in (e.g. money, people, positions)?

_____

_____

_____

_____

Nothing can fill the place in our hearts that God designed to be filled only by Him. Anything we try to put in His place is a counterfeit, a "golden calf" that leaves us void and empty.

day two

You should have identified a few "giants" in your life. If you skipped that exercise, take time now to pray about it. On the lines below, identify two "giants" that you have allowed to shrink your faith.

_____   _____

God wants us to trust Him. Pray specifically for courage and the strength to believe that God is greater than any "giants."

day three

Moses took his leadership responsibility seriously and continually interceded on behalf of the Israelites.

What about you? When you receive a prayer request, do you pray for that person earnestly? Do you remember to pray when you say you will?

All of us have forgotten a prayer request at one time or another. More times than not, we forget to pray for someone because we don't write the request down in a place where we will see it in our prayer time.

There are many ways to keep track of prayer requests. I've written requests in my calendar, in my Bible study, and on note cards attached to my car's dashboard. Regardless of the method, writing down requests is the only way I have found to actually remember to pray for the needs of others.

What method do you use to keep track of prayer requests? If you have come up with a method that works for you, share it with your small group. Write down some of the methods and ideas discussed in your small-group time.

_____
_____
_____
_____

May all of us learn to be better intercessors. God listens to our prayers just as He listened to the prayers of Moses. It is one way we can all make a difference in the lives of others.

day four

As Moses neared death, he asked God to appoint a "shepherd" for the Israelites, to lead them and guide them on their way to the Promised Land.

Our Shepherd is Jesus Christ. Like sheep, we have all gone astray (Isaiah 53:6); but when we rely on our Shepherd to guide us, we are able to stay on the course God has for us.

Read **Psalm 23**.

The "valley of the shadow of death" can also be interpreted as "the darkest valley." Have you ever experienced a time in your life that you would describe as a dark valley? If so, describe the circumstances.

_____

_____

_____

_____

In the darkest valleys we feel helpless and afraid, and often have difficulty finding our way. We learn to truly view Christ as our Shepherd.

In early 2000 I was faced with a health situation that came on suddenly and unexpectedly. Having never experienced any real health problems, I was stunned. I not only had to deal with the physical struggles, but I felt as though I had been spiritually knocked off my feet. I was deeply hurt that the Lord had allowed it to happen. Still, I knew He loved me and that He was with me.

I quoted Psalm 23 over and over, trying desperately to overcome the crippling fear that surrounded me like a dark tunnel. I spent hours in prayer on my knees before Him. The Lord spoke clearly to me through notes from friends, comments on the radio, and music. It seemed that everywhere I went, I heard references to Psalm 23. God kept letting me know that He is my Lord and my Shepherd, and that He was guiding me through the darkness.

It was during that time that Ginny Owens released a song titled "If You Want Me To."[3] In the song, she sang of being in a situation she wouldn't have chosen, yet being willing to walk forward through the valley trusting that those trials would bring her closer to her Lord, if that was what God required. Her words ministered to me and helped me put my situation into perspective. I felt as though the Lord had her record it just for me!

During the darkest periods of my valley, the Lord used music to restore my soul. The songs shifted my focus off of myself and onto Him.

We have a Shepherd who loves us more than we can imagine. He wants to comfort us with His faithful guidance and lead us in paths of righteousness.

When you are broken and your dreams are shattered, God will restore your soul. When life seems out of control, He will lead you beside quiet waters. The Lord is your Shepherd. If you follow Him, you will make it through even the darkest valleys of your life.

Next week we will follow the Israelites across the Jordan River and into the Promised Land of Canaan.

NOTE: If you haven't taken the time to redeem your coupon and order your Spiritual Identification tag, please do so now. The Spiritual Identification tag is a crucial component of the spiritual boot camp section of our study. The blessing will be worth the effort!

A Step of Faith

Have I not commanded you? Be strong and courageous.
Do not be terrified; do not be discouraged,
*for the L*ORD *your God will be with you wherever you go.*

JOSHUA 1:9

week 3 • day 1

A CALL TO LEADERSHIP

week 3 • day 2

A NEW SPIRIT

week 3 • day 3

THE CROSSING PLACE

week 3 • day 4

FAITHFUL MEMORIALS

week 3 • day 5

PERSONAL APPLICATION

A CALL TO LEADERSHIP

The Lord himself goes before you and will be with you; he will never leave you nor forsake you. Do not be afraid; do not be discouraged.
Deuteronomy 31:8

Moses told all of Israel that God would cross over into the Promised Land ahead of His people with Joshua as their new leader.

What assurance did Moses give Joshua? (**Deuteronomy 31:8**)

_____

_____

_____

_____

Now read **Deuteronomy 31:14-22**.

If Joshua wasn't shaking in his sandals before, he must have been by this time! This isn't the kind of message one wants to hear when being commissioned to leadership. God didn't say the Israelites might rebel against Him and worship idols; He said they would. Joshua was fully aware of that before he accepted his leadership position. But Joshua never lost hope that somehow the Israelites would remain faithful to the one true and living God.

For the sake of time, we won't read all of "The Song of Moses," but let's read a few verses to get a basic theme. Read **Deuteronomy 32:1-6**.

God is always upright and just. The people had been warned, yet they became a warped and crooked generation, worshiping idols and betraying their Lord. We can't imagine how Joshua must have felt as he looked upon the people with God's warning still ringing in his ears. We may not know how Joshua felt, but Moses made himself perfectly clear.

Read **Deuteronomy 32:44-47**.

With the same passion we've grown to love in him, Moses pleaded with the people to "take to heart" the words he had spoken. He implored them to command their children to obey God's law.

Fill in the blanks from **Deuteronomy 32:47** NIV:

They are not just _____ words for you— _____

_____ _____ _____.

For the Israelites to live as God intended, they needed to follow His law. Moses was about to die, yet he refused to give up on God's people. As a matter of fact, he pronounced a blessing over Israel before his death. Let's read **Deuteronomy 33:26-29**, Moses' final words to his people.

Below, fill in the blanks from verse **27** NIV:

The eternal God is your _____, and underneath

are the _____ _____.

A refuge is a shelter from danger. In times of crisis, we want to run to a place of shelter. Knowing that the Israelites were bound for rebellion and idol worship, Moses tried to help them understand that the only true shelter was in the "everlasting arms" of the almighty God.

Verse 26 refers to God as the "God of Jeshurun." This Hebrew word, meaning "upright," is a symbolic name for Israel. Moses declared that there is no one like the God of Israel; He is our divine helper, and rides on clouds in His majesty.

Read **Deuteronomy 34:1-8**.

The relationship between Moses and God was intimate. Moses had lost the privilege of entering the Promised Land, but he had not lost favor with God. The man who spoke with God "as a man speaks with his friend" was buried by God Himself. But, that's not the end of Moses' story.

Read **Matthew 17:1-3**.

Who was talking with Jesus at the transfiguration?

_____

Moses' life on earth was over, but he continues to fellowship with our Lord in heaven.

Read **Deuteronomy 34:9-12.**

Joshua had been commissioned to leadership. It must have been difficult for Joshua to follow after a leader like Moses. But in the words of Jesus Christ Himself, *"With man this is impossible, but not with God; all things are possible with God"* (**Mark 10:27**).

Are there circumstances in your life right now that seem impossible? If so, why do you feel that way?

_____
_____
_____
_____

Read **Mark 9:17-24.**

Ask God to help you overcome your unbelief.

A New Spirit

Have I not commanded you? Be strong and courageous. Do not be terrified;
do not be discouraged, for the Lord your God will be with you wherever you go.
Joshua 1:9

The older Israelites died off. Joshua and Caleb were all that remained of the generation enslaved by the Egyptians. The new generation grew accustomed to leaning on God. They were determined to trust Him and obey His commands. As we begin the Book of Joshua we will encounter a new spirit among the Israelites.

Read **Joshua 1:1-5**.

Joshua had probably grown dependent on Moses and his relationship with God. He must have felt a little overwhelmed by God's words. Yet he had been preparing for this moment his entire life.

Like Joshua, we can experience God through others for a season, but at some point in our lives it must become personal – our own relationships, our own journeys.

Several years ago, I did bookkeeping for a man we'll call Joe who owned a small business in Houston. His company had grown steadily after some difficult times in the early 1990s. His father served as his advisor in all business affairs, and even sat on his Board of Directors. They were as close as any father and son I've known.

When Joe's father died, Joe became weighted down by the burden of running the company on his own. He sought out a business partner, someone to "bounce things off of" and share in the decision-making. He met with an older gentleman who had a similar business and they began to discuss merging their companies. But, the man's company was facing some of the same difficulties Joe had overcome just a few years earlier. To have joined this man in business might have brought emotional comfort, but the cost would have been high. The burden Joe described was fear – fear of making decisions on his own, fear of uncertainty, fear of failure.

Joshua must have faced some of those same fears. The difference? Scripture indicates that Joshua took his fear to God.

Read **Joshua 1:6-9**.

"Have I not commanded you?" sounds like God was responding to objections from Joshua, doesn't it? Then God repeated Himself and told Joshua to "be strong and courageous." Interestingly, He added something new.

Fill in the blanks below from verse 9:

Have I not commanded you? Be strong and courageous. Do not be

terrified *; do not be* _discouraged_ *,*

for the Lord your God will be with you wherever you go.

When we feel afraid and discouraged, God wants us to take our burdens to Him. God didn't condemn Joshua. He encouraged him. The definition of encourage is to "give courage or resolution to."[4] Resolution means "firmness of purpose."[5] Thus, when we take our fear to God, He doesn't condemn us, He gives us courage and firmness of purpose.

My friend Joe didn't need a business partner. He needed to go to his heavenly Father and pour out his heart, then accept His counsel.

Read **Joshua 1:10-15**.

Before we proceed, let's see what Joshua was talking about when he addressed the Reubenites, Gadites, and the half-tribe of Manasseh.

Read **Numbers 32:1-6, 20-22**.

What promise did these tribes make to Moses in order to be allowed to settle in the land east of the Jordan River (**vv. 20-22**)?

_____

_____

_____

_____

_____

The Reubenites, Gadites, and half the tribe of Manasseh promised to fight alongside the rest of the Israelites. They pledged that anyone who rebelled against Joshua's commands would be put to death.

Read **Joshua 1:16-18**. In verse **18**, what was their statement to Joshua?

_____

_____

Joshua must have looked nervous! These men said they would commit to follow Joshua or die, but they wanted to make sure he was going to fulfill his end of the bargain and "be strong and courageous."

Now read all of **Joshua chapter 2**.

What a contrast to the report of Moses' day!

Based on her words in **verse 11**, what realization had Rahab come to?

_____

_____

_____

Read **James 2:24-26**.

Rahab was considered righteous in the eyes of God because she believed and acted on that belief. Rahab's actions were a testimony to her faith just as our actions testify to our faith today.

If someone were to write about your actions over the past week, would they find evidence of your faith? Why or why not?

_____

_____

_____

_____

_____

_____

Faith is the substance of things hoped for, the evidence of things not seen (**Hebrews 11:1** KJV). Rahab's faith enabled her to be courageous enough to help the spies and save her family. Rahab was a prostitute in a corrupt culture, yet she was saved by her faith. Her story is a vivid example of the abundant grace of our God.

Obviously, there was a new spirit in the Israelite camp (and in the enemy camps as well). This time, God's people would act in faith by forging ahead to claim their inheritance on the other side of the Jordan.

week 3 · day 3

THE CROSSING PLACE

The priests who carried the ark of the covenant of the Lord
stood firm on dry ground in the middle of the Jordan, while all Israel passed by
until the whole nation had completed the crossing on dry ground.
Joshua 3:17

Today we'll examine the crossing of the Jordan River and the beginning of the journey to claim the land of Canaan – an expedition this group of Israelites had waited for their entire lives.

Before we begin, let's get our bearings by identifying where the Israelites crossed the Jordan River to enter into Canaan. Locate Shittim on the map on page 8. Draw a small circle around it. We will refer to this map often as we continue to plot the Israelites' path.

After you have located Shittim, read **Joshua 3:1-6.**

The Ark of the Covenant was a sacred trunk that held the Ten Commandments. The Lord's presence dwelled above the cover, between two golden cherubim. Because God's presence was with the ark, it could only be carried by priests using special poles designed according to guidelines God gave them. By sending the ark ahead of them, the Israelites were acknowledging that it was the Lord leading them to victory.

What did Joshua tell the people to do (**v. 5**)?

_____

To *consecrate* ourselves means we set ourselves apart – body, soul, and spirit – for God's purposes. Crossing the Jordan was the fulfillment of a promise between God and His people. The experience had tremendous spiritual significance and the Israelites needed to be sanctified.

Read **Joshua 3:7-17.**

Why did God say he would exalt Joshua in the eyes of Israel (v. 7)?

_____

_____

_____

_____

At the exodus, God parted the Red Sea because it was necessary for the Israelites to escape. This miraculous event also served as a testimony of God's presence with Moses. Now, God parted the Jordan River so that the people would know He was with Joshua, just as He had been with Moses.

Joshua was commissioned to bring the Israelites into the Promised Land and distribute the land to God's people. To accomplish his task, Joshua needed the Israelites to trust his leadership, just as they had Moses'. So at the precise time the priests stepped into the river, God parted it, allowing the Israelites to cross on dry ground. This should have left no doubt in anyone's mind that Joshua was their new leader.

Look again at Joshua 3:16. Where did the Israelites cross the Jordan?

_____

On your map draw an X on the Jordan River, opposite Jericho, where the Israelites most likely crossed.

Interestingly, this wasn't the only time the Jordan had been parted in this location. Let's take a look at another occasion. Read **2 Kings 2:1-11**.

What town did Elijah and Elisha pass through when God sent Elijah to the Jordan River (vv. 4-6)? _____

God parted the waters of the Jordan for Elijah at the same basic location where Joshua and the Israelites crossed. And it was beyond the Jordan that Elijah was taken up to "heaven in a whirlwind." (**2 Kings 2:11**)

Let's look at another significant event that happened in this area of the Jordan. Read **John 1:23 34**.

According to **verse 28**, where was John baptizing? _____

John the Baptist said there was one standing among the Pharisees whose sandals he was not worthy to untie. Of course he was referring to Christ.

Now read **Matthew 3:13-17**. What event took place at the moment heaven was opened and the Spirit of God descended like a dove on Jesus?

_____

In **John 1:28**, the KING JAMES VERSION uses the word *Bethabara* instead of *Bethany:* "Bethabara beyond Jordan." It is the only time this particular name is used in Scripture. The word Bethabara is derived from a Hebrew word meaning "crossing place." Bethabara, or Bethany on the other side of the Jordan, is in the same basic area where the Israelites crossed into the Promised Land. It is also where God parted the Jordan for Elijah before Elijah was taken up to Heaven in a whirlwind. Interestingly, it is also where Jesus Christ was baptized.

This side of heaven, we may never fully understand the significance of all these events occurring in the same basic location on the Jordan River, but it certainly wasn't a coincidence.

Could it be that Jesus was baptized at the "crossing place" to symbolize the fact that through Him the waters of sin and rebellion that separate us from God were parted, giving us access to an eternal Promised Land in heaven?

Could Elijah's miraculous exit to heaven in a whirlwind from this location represent our own departure to heaven after meeting our Lord in the sky?

The Lord himself will come down from heaven, with a loud command, with the voice of the archangel and with the trumpet call of God, and the dead in Christ will rise first. After that we who are still alive and are left will be caught up together with them in the clouds to meet the Lord in the air. And so we will be with the Lord forever.
1 Thessalonians. 4:16-17

See, the LORD is coming with fire and his chariots are like a whirlwind.
Isaiah 66:15

week 3 · day 4

FAITHFUL MEMORIALS

These stones are to be a memorial to the people of Israel forever.
Joshua 4:7

God is faithful. He was faithful to free the Israelites from bondage in Egypt; He faithfully provided for their needs as they wandered in the desert for forty years; He was faithful to bring them into the Promised Land. In today's lesson, we will see the Israelites build a memorial to the faithfulness of their God.

Read **Joshua 4:1-13.**

According to **verse 7**, why were the stones set up?

_____

Why do you think God told Joshua to choose one man from each tribe to carry the stones from the Jordan?

_____

_____

It seems God was emphasizing unity. The Israelites would have to work together, every tribe, in order to claim their inheritance.

Now read **Joshua 4:14-24.**

God parted the Jordan, just as He had the Red Sea. This act exalted Joshua in the eyes of Israel and he was "revered" by the Israelites all the days of his life. According to **Joshua 4:23-24**, what other purpose did God have for parting the Jordan?

_____

_____

_____

_____

God works in our lives to bring glory to Himself. When God moves in a tangible and significant way, He reveals His power to a lost world and restores the awe of believers.

Read **Joshua 5:1-9**.

The Lord told Joshua to circumcise these young Israelite warriors. Let's see why circumcision was so important. Read **Genesis 17:1-11**.

What did the circumcision signify (**v. 11**)?

_____

Circumcision was an outward sign of the covenant between God and the descendants of Abraham, Isaac, and Jacob. God knew they were entering a land full of people who worshiped pagan gods. He wanted them to have a visible reminder, a "memorial" of their commitment to Him, as He fulfilled His covenant to give them the Promised Land.

In **Joshua 5:9**, what did God say he "rolled away" from the Israelites?

_____

Those Israelites had been reminded daily of their shame because they were uncircumcised. Circumcision identified them as God's covenant people. Before they battled against the enemies of Canaan, God rolled away the Israelites' shame and disgrace, restoring them in a tangible (and painful) way to their position as God's people. He memorialized the event by renaming that place Gilgal, which sounds like the Hebrew word for "roll." The Israelites' shame had forever been rolled away. It had been cut off and left behind.

Is there an event in your life that you would like God to roll away, cut off, and leave behind as though it never happened? If so, write a brief description.

_____
_____
_____
_____
_____
_____

Take a moment to give God access to this event. Take it before Him in complete honesty. Admit your mistakes; confess your sin. Ask Him to forgive you and roll it away. God is faithful. He will provide, and He will forgive. May today be a Gilgal for you – a day when you allow God to roll away a source of disgrace or shame.

Now read **Joshua 5:10-12**. The Israelites celebrated Passover there at the camp at Gilgal. The next day "they ate some of the produce of the land."

What happened the day after they ate this food **(vv. 11-12)**?

_____

They no longer needed the manna from heaven. The Israelites were able to eat of the produce of Canaan. God had faithfully provided for their every need.

How did God provide for their need for clothing (**Deuteronomy 29:5**)?

_____

God was faithful then, and His faithfulness continues through all generations (**Psalm 100:5**). To close today's lesson, read **Psalm 100** and spend a few moments basking in the goodness of God.

> *Shout for joy to the Lord, all the earth.*
> *Worship the Lord with gladness;*
> *Come before him with joyful songs.*
> *Know that the Lord is God.*
> *It is he who made us, and we are his;*
> *We are his people, the sheep of his pasture.*
>
> *Enter his gates with thanksgiving*
> *And his courts with praise;*
> *Give thanks to him and praise his name.*
> *For the Lord is good and his love endures forever;*
> *His faithfulness continues through all generations.*
> Psalm 100:1-5

What evidence did you find of God's faithfulness in the lessons this week?

_____

_____

_____

_____

_____

week 3 · day 5

PERSONAL APPLICATION

day one

Moses blessed the Israelites before his death. In that blessing, he reminded them that there is no one like the one true God. *The eternal God is your refuge, and underneath are the everlasting arms.* (**Deuteronomy 33:27**)

Think of the last trial you experienced. Did you run to God or to something else? How often do you seek shelter in earthy things or in people rather than resting in the everlasting arms of God? If you turned to God, use the lines below to write a prayer of thanks to Him for being your refuge and shelter in that situation. If you didn't, use these lines to write a prayer committing to turn to Him as your refuge next time.

_____

_____

_____

_____

_____

_____

_____

_____

_____

_____

day two

Joshua was fearful as he faced the challenge of leading the Israelites into the Promised Land of Canaan. But he took his fears to God. Let's review how God encouraged him.

Write **Joshua 1:9**.

Have I not commanded you, Be strong & courageous. Do not be frightened do no be discouraged. For the Lord your God will be with you wherever you go

We defined encouragement as "giving courage and firmness of purpose." How do you think God's words encouraged Joshua?

_____

Those words were recorded to encourage you too. All Scripture is written for our benefit. It is God's love letter to His people. What does **Romans 15:4** tell us about the purpose of all that is written in Scripture?

_____
give us encouragement &
endurance
Teach us to hope
_____

God's words to Joshua apply to you as well. If the Lord wants you to accomplish a task, He will gift you to do it. Take your fears and doubts to Him. Then stand on His words to you in **Joshua 1:9**.

day three

The Israelites crossed over the Jordan into the land of their inheritance in Canaan. As believers in Christ, we are reborn into a new inheritance – heaven. Let's clarify how we know we are heirs with Christ to the kingdom of heaven.

Read **Genesis 22:1-18**.

The angel of the Lord spoke with Abraham just after Abraham was willing to sacrifice his son of promise, Isaac, on the altar. God did not make Abraham actually sacrifice Isaac; it was a test of his faith. It was also a foreshadowing of God's sacrifice of Jesus, His Son of promise, on the cross for all mankind. In verse 18, the word *offspring* is translated from a Hebrew word meaning "seed." Write verse 18, replacing the word *offspring* with the word *seed*.

_____
_____
_____
_____
_____

Now read **Galatians 3:15-16, 29**. What is the relevancy of God's covenant with Abraham to you as a believer in Christ?

_____

_____

_____

_____

_____

Read **Romans 8:15-17**.

Christ is the Seed through which the promise to Abraham was fulfilled. The greatest inheritance of Abraham's descendants was God Himself. When we believe in Christ, we become co-heirs with Christ to the ultimate Promised Land – heaven.

day four

When God memorialized the parting of the Jordan, He had one man from each tribe select a stone from the river. To claim their inheritance, the Israelites would have to be unified and work together as they fought their enemy.

Read **Psalm 133**. What does this Psalm tell you about unity?

_____

_____

_____

_____

God desires unity among His people. Let's take a look at an example of unity among Christians.

Read **Acts 2:42-47**.

Do you have a group of people with whom you eat with a glad and sincere heart, praising God and enjoying fellowship? If so, it is a wonderful blessing from God. Enjoy it, and protect it. It is like a precious slice of heaven on earth.

THE BATTLE BEGINS

The wages of sin is death, but the gift of God is eternal life
in Christ Jesus our Lord.

ROMANS 6:23

week 4 • day 1

FAITHFUL MARCH

week 4 • day 2

STUNNED BY DEFEAT

week 4 • day 3

THE WAGES OF SIN

week 4 • day 4

CITY OF PALMS

week 4 • day 5

PERSONAL APPLICATION

FAITHFUL MARCH

*By faith the walls of Jericho fell, after the people had marched
around them for seven days.*
Hebrews 11:30

This week we will examine the battles the Israelites fought to gain possession of their Promised Land. The first is the famous battle at Jericho. This city was the gateway to Canaan. To claim the rest of the land, Joshua needed a victory in Jericho. Our lesson today begins as the Israelites approached Jericho, where Joshua had a significant encounter.

Read **Joshua 5:13-15**. In **verse 15**, what did the "commander" tell Joshua to do?

_____

Let's take a closer look at this "commander of the Lord's army." We'll begin by determining who he was not. Read **Revelation 19:6-10**.

When John (the author of Revelation) fell at the angel's feet to worship, what did the angel say?

_____

An angel would never have allowed Joshua to worship him. So we can confidently conclude this "commander of the Lord's army" was not an angel.

Let's see what clues we can find in Scripture as to the identity of this commander.

Read **Revelation 19:11-16**.

The armies of heaven were following the rider of the white horse. According to **verse 13**, what was His name? _____

What was written on His robe and His thigh (**v. 16**)?

_____

According to **John 1:14-17**, who is the Word that became flesh?

_____

_____

So, based on these scriptures, who was this "commander of the Lord's army"?

_____

_____

Jesus Christ pre-incarnate was the commander who stood before Joshua. Joshua took off his sandals and worshiped Him. Joshua was in the presence of the one and only Son of God, the Commander of the armies of heaven. As we will see, He led Joshua and the Israelites to victory at this very first battle to claim their inheritance.

Read **Joshua 6:1-5**.

How many days did the Lord tell Joshua to march around the walls of Jericho? ____

This was a strange set of instructions. Why would the Israelites march around the city for days rather than simply attack? Undoubtedly, this was a test of their obedience and patience. But Joshua received these instructions straight from the Lord Himself, and he didn't question. He faithfully carried out those instructions, marching around the city one time each day for six days.

Read **Joshua 6:8-21**.

On the seventh day, the Israelites marched around the city seven times. At the proper time, there was a shout, and the walls of Jericho collapsed. Joshua carried out the Lord's instructions to the letter. He believed the Lord would do as He promised. What military leader would conduct a battle in this manner unless he believed that the Lord Himself would topple those walls?

What does **Hebrews 11:30** tell us caused the walls to fall? _____

_____

Their faith was rewarded and the men charged in, killing all who were in the city, even the livestock. Let's see if we can gain a little insight into the reasons God would call for such destruction.

Read **Deuteronomy 13:12-16**.

Historians have uncovered evidence of the sinful culture of the Canaanites. Their temples featured prostitutes, orgies, and human sacrifice. Their gods delighted in butchery and sadism. Archaeologists have found a great number of jars containing the tiny bones of children who were sacrificed to Baal. Families seeking good luck in a new home would kill one of their children and seal the body in the mortar of the wall. In many ways, Canaan could be compared to Sodom and Gomorrah.[6]

Read **Joshua 6:22-27**.

The Israelites burned the entire city of Jericho to the ground, but Rahab and her family were spared.

Joshua placed a curse over the ruined city of Jericho. What were to be the consequences of trying to rebuild the city?

_____

_____

_____

The curse was fulfilled about 500 years later. According to **1 Kings 16:34**, who rebuilt Jericho? What price did he pay?

_____

_____

Let's update the Israelites' journey on our map. Using a red pen or map pencil, draw a line from the X at the Jordan River to Gilgal, where the Israelites camped. Then draw a line to Jericho. Using a blue map pencil, place an X over the city of Jericho. We'll use blue Xs to track the Israelites' battles.

The story of the Israelites marching around the walls of Jericho is depicted in children's videos and taught in most children's Sunday school classes. It is a story of obedience, patience, and faith in God. The Israelites had to trust God to bring them victory, even though the method couldn't be reasoned out.

Take a moment to ask God if there are any battles you are trying to win by your own methods. If something comes to mind, write down the circumstances on the lines below. Spend some time reflecting on the situation. Ask God to reveal any wrong motives or attitudes that might be hindering your victory.

_____

_____

_____

_____

_____

_____

_____

_____

Would you have followed the strange instructions Joshua received? Do you think you would have believed God would topple those walls as the priests shouted? What do your answers say about your level of faith in God? Spend the remainder of the day reflecting on your level of obedience.

STUNNED BY DEFEAT

Joshua tore his clothes and fell facedown to the ground before the
ark of the Lord, remaining there till evening.
Joshua 7:6

Begin today by reading **Joshua 7:1-9.**

What does verse 1 say the Israelites did regarding the devoted things?

_____

The Hebrew word translated "acted unfaithfully" is *ma'al*. It means "to cover up, to act secretly, to betray or sin against."

According to **Joshua 6:17-19,** what were the devoted things?

_____

What were God's specific instructions concerning these devoted things?

_____

What did God say would happen to Israel if they did not follow His instructions concerning the devoted things?

_____

Achan betrayed God by secretly taking some items. After such a successful battle at Jericho, the Israelites were stunned by their defeat at Ai. It was a humiliating loss.

According to **Joshua 7:6,** what was Joshua's response?

_____

Joshua expressed his grief be tearing his clothes. He sought to understand what had happened. If this seems familiar to you, it is because we witnessed Joshua tearing his clothes when the Israelites had refused to fight for their Promised Land forty years earlier.

Read **Numbers 14:1-3**. What question had the Israelites asked that prompted Joshua and Caleb to tear their clothes (**v. 3**)?

_____

_____

_____

_____

What question did Joshua ask the Lord (**Joshua 7:7**)?

_____

_____

_____

_____

Ironic, isn't it? Joshua uttered the same words of disbelief that grieved him forty years earlier. Often, we can easily see a lack of faith in others, but then the same words come rolling out of our own mouths sometime later. Can you recall a time when you spoke words of disbelief that you had never thought you'd say? If so, describe the circumstances.

_____

_____

_____

_____

Joshua tore his clothes, and he and the elders of Israel fell facedown, sprinkling dust on their heads. This custom was usually accompanied by prayers of confession and worship. They spent the rest of the day before the Lord, humbling themselves and asking God to reveal what had caused their defeat.

Their biggest mistake had been failing to seek God's direction before the battle at Ai. Had they done so, they would have realized the Lord wasn't with them. They could have become aware of Achan's sin beforehand, and avoided the whole messy ordeal.

The Hebrew name *Achan* means "trouble." Do you think Achan might have been in trouble before? His sin at Jericho was remembered always and was even used to describe him in **1 Chronicles 2:7**. Write the description of Achan (listed as Akar) in this passage.

_____

The book of Chronicles is a family record of sorts. It's a precious memorial of God's people and Israel's heritage. Imagine being remembered for bringing trouble on your family and violating God's laws!

Tomorrow we will read the rest of Achan's story. Allow a few extra minutes to complete the lesson because we will set aside some special prayer time and take a few minutes to offer our praise to God and worship Him.

week 4 · day 3

THE WAGES OF SIN

The wages of sin is death, but the gift of God is eternal life in Christ Jesus our Lord.
Romans 6:23

Yesterday, we saw the humiliating defeat of the Israelites at Ai. Joshua and the elders were grief-stricken and stunned by the defeat. When we last saw Joshua, he and the elders were facedown before the Lord. Joshua was struggling with doubt and fear.

Read **Joshua 7:10-26**.

As I read the account of Achan's death, along with his family, my heart ached. I wanted to read that God forgave Achan after he told Joshua where to find the devoted things. I wanted him to be given a second chance. As I asked God to help me understand this heartbreaking scene, He brought to mind **Romans 6:23**. Reread it at the top of the page.

I related far more with Achan than I wanted to admit. We often try to rationalize what we consider "small sins," don't we? But God told the Israelites that they were to totally destroy everything in Jericho. Can't you imagine Achan thinking no one would know if he only took a few things? What harm would it do?

Without Christ, we deserve to be at the bottom of that heap of stones with Achan and his family. What does **Romans 3:23** tell us? _____

_____

There are no "small sins." If we don't believe that our sins are punishable by death, we cheapen the sacrifice Jesus made on the Cross. Christ did more than die that brutal death for us, He died instead of us. He died the death that we deserved.

We celebrate the grace of God. We teach our children that Jesus loves them. But do we embrace the truth that God is holy and just, and that He demands obedience?

I remember talking to my son one day about some undesirable behavior. I told him I was concerned about his apparent lack of fear for God. His response gave me chills. "Am I supposed to be afraid of God?" he asked honestly.

We serve a gracious and compassionate God. But He is also holy, and He will not be in the presence of sin. Sin separates us from God and destroys our relationship with Him. If we continue living in a pattern of sin, we will experience the discipline of a just and holy God.

Achan took the devoted things. His punishment was death, not only for himself, but for his entire family. It is hard to read a passage like this one, but it can help us to better comprehend the gift of God in His Son.

Read **Romans 8:1-4** and write verse 1.

_____

_____

_____

_____

_____

Christ accepted the punishment that was rightly due you and me. Because of His sacrifice we are no longer condemned. We have the opportunity to live for all eternity in heaven. God gave us incredible mercy by pardoning our sins. He displayed abundant grace by giving us the precious gift of eternal life.

I asked you to set aside a little extra time to complete today's lesson in order to have a special prayer time. I hope you have done that. If not, try to make time for this part of the lesson sometime this week.

Begin with a time of confession.

Ask God for forgiveness for specific sins you have struggled with recently. Confess anything you have done that you know is not His will. Look up the Scriptures listed below during this time.

Romans 3:23   **1 John 1:9**   **Acts 13:38-39**   **Colossians 1:13-14**

Read **Psalm 130** as a prayer to God.

Now spend a few moments thanking God for the gift of His Son. Some scriptures are listed to assist you.

Romans 5:6-8   **Psalm 30**   **Colossians 3:15-17**   **Psalm 100**

Write **Hebrews 13:15**.

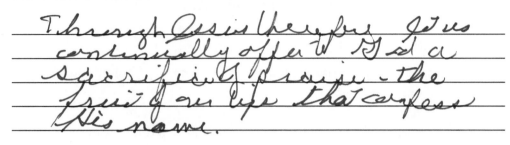

Through Jesus therefore let us continually offer to God a sacrifice of praise - the fruit of our lips that confess His name.

Read **Psalm 149:1-4** aloud.

Spend time listening to Christian music – Gospel, contemporary, praise and worship, whatever speaks to your spirit. Choose a time when no one is around and sing the lyrics straight to the heart of God. Rejoice in your Maker; be glad in your King! Praise His name with dancing, for He delights in you. Offer Him the sacrifice of praise.

Conclude by reading **Psalm 150** aloud.

week 4 • day 4

CITY OF PALMS

They took palm branches and went out to meet him shouting Hosanna!
Blessed is he who comes in the name of the Lord! Blessed is the King of Israel!
John 12:13

At this point in our study, the Israelites have entered the land of Canaan. Today's lesson will focus on the symbolism of this territory God promised to His people.

As the Israelites crossed the Jordan, Jericho was considered the gateway to their land of promise. This "Promised Land" was a foreshadowing of our eternal home in heaven.

What is the city of Jericho called in **Deuteronomy 34:1-3** and **2 Chronicles 28:15**?

_____

Jericho was considered the gateway to the promised land. Let's see what Scripture says about the gates of heaven.

Ezekiel 40-48 records a vision of a temple where the presence of God would dwell. The first tabernacle and the temples were representations of the true sanctuary in heaven (**Hebrews 8:5**). Take a look at this vision in **Ezekiel 40:1-7, 16, 34**. With what were the walls of the gates decorated?

_____

There is another time when palm trees (or branches) are mentioned in Scripture.

Read **John 12:12-13**.

Have you ever wondered why the people of Jerusalem were waving palm branches as Jesus entered the city at the triumphal entry? Palm branches represented victory, triumph, and royalty. Those palm branches represented God's promise to fulfill His covenant with Israel.

The Jewish people were watching for a Messiah. Take a moment to read what the prophets said about the Messiah.

Read **Isaiah 11:1**. What did Isaiah say the Branch would do? _____

_____

Now read **Jeremiah 23:1-3**. What does verse 3 say the flock (God's people) would do when God gathers them back to His pasture?

_____

Read **Leviticus 26:3, 9**. What was the reward the Lord promised the Israelites if they obeyed His commands?

_____

Read **Genesis 17:1-8**. What covenant promises did God make to Abraham's descendants? (**Genesis 17:6**)

_____

Have you noticed the common thread in theses verses? The Israelites were expecting to be fruitful and to be blessed. To them, palm trees, along with their branches, represented fruitfulness and blessings provided by God.[7]

God's people had been promised they would be blessed and fruitful. They were expecting a king to rise up from David's lineage who would fulfill that promise. Those people knew the words of the prophets, and as they waved those palm branches, they anticipated that Jesus was the One.

Look back at **John 12:13** and fill in the blanks.

> *They took palm branches and went out to meet him* _____
> *Hosanna! Blessed is he who comes in the name of the Lord!*
> *Blessed is* _____ _____ _____ _____.

These people were passionate. Their shouts proclaimed their belief that Jesus was the long-awaited King.

Picture Jesus riding through the gates of Jerusalem on that donkey amidst the shouts of the people acknowledging Him as King! Imagine the people looking into His eyes as He passed, all of them understanding the significance of those palm branches. They were symbolic – a silent and powerful testimony of the people's faith in God's covenant, and in Jesus as the One through whom God would fulfill it.

Now read **Revelation 7:9-10**. What were the people holding in their hands?

_____

Inside the gates of heaven, we will stand before the throne and wave our palm branches. We will celebrate our fruitfulness and the victory of the ultimate and true fulfillment of God's blessed covenant.

God says that He "will wipe every tear" from our eyes (**Revelation 21:4**) in that Holy City. I hope He plans to provide a multitude of tissues. I cannot possibly imagine waving my palm without tears streaming down my face! Just as the people at the triumphal entry almost two thousand years ago looked into the eyes of their King, we too will see our Savior, the King of kings and Lord of lords, face to face.

week 4 · day 5

PERSONAL APPLICATION

day one

When we are around someone who opposes us, or even launches personal attacks, our immediate instinct is to fight. But if we act before seeking God's direction, we may find ourselves in a battle we weren't prepared for, just as the Israelites had been at Ai.

At Jericho, Joshua sought the Lord's guidance before acting. God told him to march around the city for six days without going to war. The Israelites inhabited the land and paraded around the city for a full week before attacking.

Although God's methods were certainly unconventional, by carefully following His instructions, Joshua was victorious. He waited until the appointed time to launch his attack.

You were asked to identify a battle you have been trying to win using your own methods. Now let's go a step further. Take that battle before God and sincerely seek His counsel. If this is the first time you've taken this matter before God, do you sense any changes you need to make in your battle strategy? Have you been over-confident in your ability to handle the problem, the way the Israelites were at Ai? Record your thoughts.

_____

_____

_____

_____

_____

_____

_____

_____

_____

_____

If you *have* taken this battle before God previously, were you completely obedient to what you sensed God telling you to do? Again, record your thoughts.

_____
_____
_____
_____
_____
_____
_____

Sometimes, we act hastily. God might want us to walk around the issue for a while as He prepares us and adjusts our hearts. If we are having a conflict with another person, perhaps our reactions are fueling his or her behavior. If our battle is against an area of weakness such as an addiction, God may want us to rest in Him and allow Him to strengthen and change us so we can win the battle.

The only way we can achieve victory in the many battles of this life is to use God's methods. Those methods may not always make sense, but they will bring victory. We have to trust God enough to obey Him, even if we don't understand the instructions. He may just topple a few walls on your behalf!

day two

Achan was remembered for the trouble he brought on Israel. Any good he had done in his lifetime was overshadowed by his greed and disobedience at Ai.

Achar, who brought trouble on Israel by violating the ban on taking devoted things.
1 Chronicles 2:7

If a "chronicle" were to be written about your life, what would you like to be written?

_____
_____
_____
_____
_____
_____
_____

Ask God to help you make your answer to this question a reality in your life.
Write a prayer of commitment.

_____
_____
_____
_____
_____
_____
_____

day three

The wages of sin is death. Jesus accepted the wages for our sin when He died on the Cross. The suffering He endured on the Cross was horrific. Let's explore the physical pain Christ endured when He accepted the punishment for our sins.

According to **Mark 15:15**, what happened to Jesus before He was crucified?

_____

In *A Case for Christ*, Lee Strobel gives graphic details of a Roman flogging.

> Roman floggings were known to be terribly brutal. They usually consisted of thirty-nine lashes, but frequently were a lot more. The soldier would use a whip of braided leather thongs with metal balls woven into them. When the whip would strike the flesh, these balls would cause deep bruises or contusions, which would break open with further blows. The back would be so shredded that part of the spine was sometimes exposed. The whipping would have gone all the way from the shoulders down to the back, the buttocks, and the back of the legs.[8]

After flogging Him, the soldiers put a purple robe on Jesus and made a crown of thorns for His head. They mocked him because people called him "King of the Jews." According to Mark 15:20, what happened to Jesus after the soldiers finished mocking him?

_____

Let's take a moment to absorb the agony Christ endured on the cross. The following details about the crucifixion are taken from *The Case for Christ*.

> The Romans used spikes that were five to seven inches long and tapered to a sharp point. They were driven through the wrists. This was a solid position that would lock the hand (that was considered part of the hand in the language of the day). The nail would go through the place where the median nerve runs. This is the largest nerve going out of the hand, and it would be crushed by the nail. At this point Jesus was hoisted as the crossbar was attached to the vertical stake, and then nails were driven through Jesus' feet. Again, the nerves in his feet would have been crushed, again causing excruciating pain. His arms would have immediately been stretched, probably about six inches in length, and both shoulders would have become dislocated. Once a person is hanging in the vertical position, crucifixion is essentially an agonizingly slow death by asphyxiation. [9]

A number of devoted women stood near the cross as Jesus died (**John 19:25**). Imagine for a moment that you are standing among them, watching Jesus. If you could say something to Him as He hangs there in pain, accepting your punishment, what would you say? Record your words.

_____

_____

_____

_____

_____

_____

_____

As Jesus hung on that Cross, He knew what you'd say. He died that brutal death on the Cross for you.

day four

In Day Four we explored the possibility that the palm trees, along with their braches, represented fruitfulness and blessings provided by God.

What does **Psalm 92:12** say about the righteous?

_____

According to **Romans 3:22**, where does righteousness come from?

_____

When we accept Jesus as our Savior by faith, we are made righteous through His blood that was shed on the cross. His willingness to die for our sins enables us to come into a place of right standing with God. We are able to bear fruit and flourish like palm trees planted in the courts of our God. It is a loving gift from a merciful Savior.

To close this week, spend a few moments offering Jesus a sacrifice of praise and thanksgiving for His willingness to endure the Cross for you. That's how much your Jesus loves you!

LESSONS FROM THE TRENCHES

Know therefore that the Lord your God is God; he is the faithful God,
keeping his covenant of love to a thousand generations
of those who love him and keep his commands.

DEUTERONOMY 7:9

week 5 • day 1

A SECOND CHANCE

week 5 • day 2

OUR FAITHFUL GOD

week 5 • day 3

THE GIBEONITE DECEPTION

week 5 • day 4

THE SUN STANDS STILL

week 5 • day 5

PERSONAL APPLICATION

A Second Chance

The Lord said to Joshua, "Do not be afraid; do not be discouraged.
Take the whole army with you, go up and attack Ai.
For I have delivered into your hands the king of Ai, his people, his city and his land."
Joshua 8:1

We left off last week with the defeat of the Israelites at Ai. Joshua had not sought the Lord's guidance before entering this battle the first time. In this second attempt, Joshua was careful not to make the same mistake.

Describe a time when you experienced defeat because you didn't inquire of the Lord before acting.

_____

_____

_____

_____

_____

_____

What do you believe God would have instructed you to do?

_____

_____

_____

_____

Joshua must have spent much time in prayer before the events in chapter eight ever began. At its opening, He is receiving words of encouragement from God.

Read **Joshua 8:1**. God used similar words to encourage Joshua when he first took over for Moses (**Joshua 1:9**). Joshua had underestimated the people of Ai. This time, Joshua listened as God told him to take the whole army into battle. Joshua followed His instructions carefully, just as he had in Jericho. As a result, today we will witness their victory!

Read **Joshua 8:2-9.** In verse 2, what did God say the Israelites could take from the city this time?

_____ and _____

How ironic. Had Achan suppressed his greediness, he could have taken much more just a short time later, with God's blessing.

Now read **Joshua 8:10-29.** What does verse **18** tell us the Lord told Joshua to do?

_____

How long did Joshua hold out the javelin (**v. 26**)?

_____

Joshua stood there holding that javelin. He didn't dare drop it. Do you remember what lesson Joshua learned at the first battle he fought? (See page 20)

Look back at **Exodus 17:11-13.**

Moses changed Joshua's name as a lasting memorial, reminding him the Lord is the One who brings victory in battle. Joshua remembered. He held that javelin out until every last person had been destroyed.

What does **Joshua 8:29** tell us Joshua did to the king of Ai?

_____

_____

The large pile of rocks over the king's body probably served as a memorial to signify what would happen if the people turned away from God. Joshua knew the Israelites would turn from the Lord and worship the idols of Canaan. God had told him so. Yet Joshua took every opportunity to remind the people of the importance of obedience and loyalty to the one true God.

What are some "idols" that our society worships?

_____

_____

_____

_____

_____

_____

Unless our society turns from those idols to the Lord, we will receive judgment. Take a moment to pray for our nation to turn away from useless things and place their trust in God.

Leaving the king's body at the city gates may have symbolized God's judgment. In Old Testament times, civil law cases were often heard at the gateway to a city. Either the elders or the king would dispense justice at this location.[10]

Sometimes we think one failure is an indication we aren't doing what God has called us to do. Joshua was so shaken by his failure that he was overcome by doubt and disbelief. But he took his doubt and fear to God and he was given a second chance. Once again, Joshua was strengthened by God's words and found the courage to go forward, believing God would do as He promised.

Have you failed in a recent situation? If so, how can you relate to Joshua?

_____

_____

_____

_____

Maybe you forgot to seek God first for guidance. Or perhaps you were determined to make things happen your way. Or maybe you were just overly zealous and got off track.

Spend a few minutes in prayer and ask God to confirm to you what He desires for you to do. Then ask Him for the courage to trust Him and try again.

He is a God of second chances!

week 5 · day 2

OUR FAITHFUL GOD

Know therefore that the Lord your God is God; he is the faithful God,
keeping his covenant of love to a thousand generations of those who love him
and keep his commands.
Deuteronomy 7:9

Before we continue with our study, let's update your map. Draw a red line from Jericho to Ai, then to Bethel. Place a blue X between Ai and Bethel, west of Ai as described in **Joshua 8:9.**

Now read **Joshua 8:30-35.** According to **verse 33,** why did Joshua gather the Israelites in this place?

_____

What did Joshua copy onto the stones (**v. 32**)?

_____

Joshua was following Moses' instructions. Let's take a look at what Moses said. Read **Deuteronomy 27:1-8.**

Hold your place in Deuteronomy and look again at **Joshua 8:33.** According to this verse, how were the Israelites positioned on the mountains?

_____

_____

_____

_____

Look at the following illustration below. Read **Deuteronomy 27: 9-13** and fill in the names of the tribes as they stood on the mountains according to the instructions in these verses.

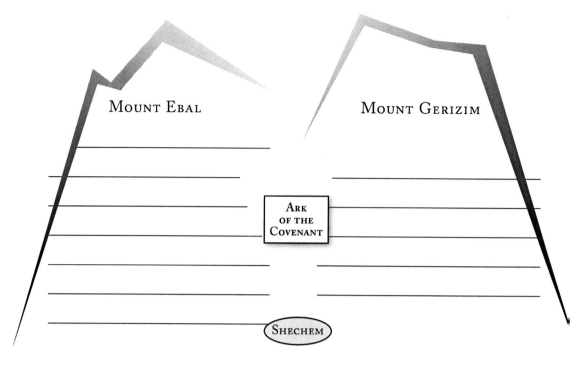

This was the positioning of the Israelites as the blessings and the curses were recited. They stood in front of those mountains facing the Ark of the Covenant, prepared to hear the law that God gave Moses on Mt. Sinai.

When I first looked at the arrangement of the Israelites, I wondered how they could have heard the law being recited. After all, they didn't have loud speakers or sound equipment. Interestingly, upon further research I discovered that these two mountains form a huge natural amphitheater, which still exists today. It allowed the Israelites to hear every word clearly.[11] Isn't that incredible? God directed His people to the one place where they could all gather together and hear the law proclaimed.

God often creates circumstances that enable us to hear what He has to say. Can you recall a time when you were convinced God had placed you in a particular situation just so that you would be able hear a message from Him? If so, briefly explain.

_____

_____

_____

_____

_____

_____

_____

_____

Take a moment to thank Him for His faithful provision.

Read **Deuteronomy 27:15-28:14** and try to visualize this event as you read through some of the blessings and curses.

I love the way the people said "Amen" at the reading of each curse. The word *Amen* is a Hebrew word meaning "truly, so be it – truth." Did you notice the blessings weren't written in the same format? The people didn't say "Amen" after each blessing. They could have gotten quite rowdy shouting "Amen" to each blessing they would receive for obedience. But it required submission for them to say "Amen" after the reading of the curses. The Israelites were making a public profession of their acceptance of the law before God.

The city of Shechem is included in the illustration on the previous page. This particular area of Canaan had great significance to the Israelites.

Read **Genesis 12:1-7**. According to verse 6, where was Abraham when God first promised the land of Canaan to his descendants?

_____

What did Abraham build at Shechem (**v. 7**)?

_____

Now read **Genesis 33:18-20**.

What did Jacob purchase from the sons of Hamor?

_____

_____

_____

_____

Some of this land rightly belonged to the Israelites. Jacob had purchased it many years earlier. What name did Jacob give the altar he built here?

_____

El Elohe Israel means "the mighty God of Israel." And what a mighty God He is!

This was the location where God had first promised Abraham this land. As Joshua built his altar, he must have reflected on God's faithfulness to fulfill this promise.

There were many battles yet to come for the Israelites. This time at the mountains probably renewed their sense of purpose and reminded them of God's faithfulness.

He is a faithful God who keeps His covenant of love to…those who love him and keep his commands.

Deuteronomy 7:9

week 5 · day 3

GIBEONITE DECEPTION

Then Joshua made a treaty of peace with them to let them live,
and the leaders of the assembly ratified it by oath.
Joshua 9:15

In yesterday's lesson, we learned that Joshua carefully followed Moses' instructions by building an altar and reciting the law at Mount Ebal and Mount Gerizim. God had gathered the Israelites at the same location where He first promised the land to Abraham's descendants.

With their thoughts directed toward the faithfulness of their Almighty God, and a renewed awareness of the blessings for obedience or consequences for disobedience, the Israelites were ready to continue their journey to claim their inheritance.

After the ceremony in the mountains, the Israelites returned to their camp at Gilgal. Word of their victories spread throughout the region. The Canaanites began to recognize that the Lord was indeed with the Israelites.

Read **Joshua 9:1-6**. What does verse 4 say the Gibeonites resorted to?

_____

They loaded their donkeys with worn-out sacks and old wineskins that had cracked and had been mended. They wore tattered sandals and old clothes. Their bread was dry and moldy. Can you imagine what a sight these men must have been as they entered the camp at Gilgal?

The Gibeonites came straight to the point. What did they ask Joshua to do (**v. 6**)?

_____

The Hebrew word translated "treaty" here is *beriyth*. It can also mean "a compact, covenant, league, or treaty." The first time this word appears in Scripture is when God made a covenant with Noah to spare his family from the flood. The next was when God promised to never again destroy the earth with a flood (**Genesis 9:9-11**). A covenant is very serious in the eyes of God. It cannot be broken.

The Gibeonites, also called Hivites, were descendants of Noah's son Ham, who had experienced that first covenant. They knew that a covenant was a solemn, binding agreement. That's why they would rather have entered into a covenant with the children of Israel than fight them. A covenant gave them protection.[12]

Read **Joshua 9:7-15**. According to **verse 14**, what major mistake did Joshua make in dealing with the Gibeonites?

_____

Joshua had done it again. Don't we often do the same thing? We think we have the wisdom to handle a situation, so we make a decision without first consulting the Lord.

These guys must have been incredible actors. It's difficult to believe that all Joshua did to verify the authenticity of the Gibeonites' story was "sample their provisions." In no time at all, he made a covenant with the Gibeonites, thus binding the Israelites to peace with them forever.

God had clearly instructed the Israelites not to make treaties with the people of Canaan. Moses had recorded the instructions in Deuteronomy (the book of the law that Joshua had just read to the people in the mountains). Let's see what God's instructions were.

Read **Deuteronomy 7:1-2** and **20:10-18**. What did God say the Israelites were to do to the people of Canaan?

_____

How were they to treat cities that did not belong to the nations nearby?

_____

_____

_____

Why do you think God had the Israelites deal so differently with people from distant lands?

_____

_____

The Gibeonites knew that if they pretended to be from a land "at a distance" they would be offered peace. Their ruse worked exactly as they planned.

Read **Joshua 9:16-27**.

What did the Israelites learn three days after they had made this treaty?

_____

_____

Joshua and the Israelites were certainly angry when they discovered they had been deceived. Yet they didn't attack because of the covenant they had sworn by the Lord.

When the Israelites grumbled, no excuses were given. The leaders simply stated the facts. What do you think Joshua might have said when he went before the Lord after realizing his costly mistake?

_____

_____

_____

_____

Among other things, he probably asked for forgiveness. But this was one of those times when the consequences for the mistake were not wiped away with God's forgiveness.

Can you recall a situation in your life when consequences for sin remained even though you had received God's forgiveness?

_____

_____

_____

_____

Joshua made the Gibeonites slaves. What tasks did he assign them (**v. 27**)?

_____

_____

_____

_____

God had made it clear that the Israelites would suffer consequences if they failed to completely destroy the people in Canaan. Joshua's heart must have been heavy as he considered the future of his people.

Look back over **Deuteronomy 20:18**. What did God say these people would teach the Israelites?

_____

_____

_____

_____

Perhaps Joshua made the Gibeonites serve at the Tent of Meeting in an attempt to protect the Israelites from some of the consequences of his sin. He might have even hoped the Israelites would influence the Gibeonites rather than the reverse. By working at the Tent of Meeting, the Gibeonites would have been continually exposed to the one true God.

week 5 · day 4

THE SUN STANDS STILL

The Lord said to Joshua, "Do not be afraid of them; I have given them into your hand
Not one of them will be able to withstand you."
Joshua 10:8

The covenant Joshua made with the Gibeonites required the Israelites not only
to be at peace with them, but also to protect them. Their alliance caught the
attention of the king of Jerusalem, which was located about five miles southeast
of Gibeon. The king joined forces with other major cities within Canaan to
attack the Israelites.

Read **Joshua 10:1-7.**

On your map, locate the cities involved in this attack. The military troops moved
in, each from their own city. They represented a large force within Canaan.
Joshua needed to win this battle. Victory would enable the Israelites to penetrate
deep into the heart of the Promised Land. But a loss would undermine the
entire mission.

What were the Lord's words to Joshua (**10:8**)?

_____

_____

_____

_____

God is faithful, even when we are not. Joshua had been warned not to make a
treaty with the people of Canaan. God had told him that allowing Canaanites to
live among His people would cause them to eventually turn away and worship
other gods. He had made a huge mistake in making a treaty with Gibeon, yet
God was with him and encouraged him to continue. Don't you just love that
about God? Joshua's mistake would have lasting repercussions. Yet God was still
faithful to fulfill His promises.

Read Joshua **10:9-15**.

The Israelites marched all night from Gilgal to Gibeon. The Lord threw the Canaanites "into confusion before Israel," but Joshua could see they needed more time. If the Canaanites had the opportunity to regroup overnight, they would be much more of a threat to the sleep-deprived Israelites.

What request did Joshua make of the Lord in **verse 12**?

_____

_____

_____

_____

God granted Joshua's request and the daylight was miraculously extended an extra twenty-four hours. The God Who created the heavens and the earth can summon the earth to slow down if He pleases. Science says this is impossible; yet it happened.

Read **Psalm 50:1** below.

> *The Mighty One, God, the Lord, speaks and summons the earth*
> *from the rising of the sun to the place where it sets.*

How does the information we just read challenge you personally?

_____

_____

_____

_____

Could it be that God chose to take this particular action not only to allow the Israelites to achieve victory, but also to send a strong message to them?

Read **Deuteronomy 4:19**. What did God caution the Israelites not to worship?

_____

_____

God has a purpose in everything He does; nothing is insignificant. The sun and moon were principal deities among the Canaanites.[13] Here, at the prayer of Joshua, the Canaanites saw the very objects of their worship obey the Lord of the Israelites. From the hailstones to the lingering sun, this entire battle served to testify that the Lord was fighting for Israel.

What evidence of God's faithfulness did you find through the lessons this week?

_____

_____

_____

_____

Update your map by placing a blue X at Gibeon and Beth Horon; at Azekah and Makkedah. Draw a red line from Bethel to Gibeon.

week 5 · day 5

PERSONAL APPLICATION

day one

Joshua and the Israelites were given a second chance to be victorious in battle at Ai. When Joshua took his fear to God, he was given a second chance.

Has there ever been a time in your life when you failed publicly as Joshua did? If so, did you take your discouragement to God or did you seek the "wisdom" of other people?

_____

_____

_____

_____

God wants us to take our failure, our discouragement, and our pain to Him. Sometimes, like Joshua, we fail because we forget to consult God before acting. Our failure might be caused by disobedience or sin, or it may happen just because we are tired and worn out.

Read **Matthew 11:28-30**. Jesus sits at the right hand of the Father, and He longs for you to come to Him when you are weary and burdened. What does He say He will give you (**v. 28**)?

_____

_____

_____

_____

The Greek word translated here as "rest" is _anapausis_. It means "intermission." Has there ever been a period in your life when you just wanted to take a break?

Jesus Christ offers us an "intermission" from the burdens and duties that wear us down. He is gentle and humble in heart (**v. 29**). Someone who is "humble in heart" is easy to talk to. Have you experienced Christ that way? _____

Stop right now and take an intermission. Find a quiet place with no distractions (maybe your bedroom or the backyard). Get on your knees and pour out your heart to your Savior and Friend. Let Him lavish His gentle love upon you as you lay your burdens at His feet. You will truly find rest for your soul.

day two

Look back at **Joshua 8:30-31**. What types of offerings did Joshua make on the altar at Mount Ebal?

_____ and _____

The purpose of the burnt offering was to cover sin. Let's take a look at the fellowship offering. The Hebrew words *zabach shelem* mean "to sacrifice in thanks." This was an offering to thank God for all He had done and all that He was going to do.

When you receive a blessing from God, offer it back to Him by sharing it with others. God's activity in your life is intended to bring Him glory. If you keep it to yourself, you will miss the chance to make it a blessing to others. If God blesses you financially, give Him a thank offering above and beyond your tithe. If He reveals Himself to you through circumstances in your life, tell everyone who will listen. If He blesses you with an exceptional talent, use it to build up His kingdom and bring Him glory.

Describe something that God has done in your life recently that you need to offer back to Him as a thank offering.

_____
_____
_____
_____

Take a few moments to praise Him for His activity in your life. Then share it!

day three

The Gibeonites deceived Joshua into thinking they were from a distant land in order to establish a treaty (or covenant) of peace with the Israelites. They knew that a peace treaty would bring them protection. Their lives were spared, but their deception resulted in a life of bondage as woodcutters and water carriers.

Read **Proverbs 12:19** and **20:17**.

The Gibeonites tasted the momentary sweetness of their successful ruse, but it soon turned to a mouth full of gravel. They thought they would gain life and freedom by using deception. But true freedom is gained only by truth. Sometimes deception seems easier at first, but it always leads to bondage of one form or another.

Whether we are the deceiver or the deceived, deception has consequences. Even using exaggerations to enhance a story, or telling a lie to protect your image is deception.

Read **Galatians 5:1**.

Deception results in a yoke of slavery. It may be slavery to the fear of being discovered, slavery to the pressure to continually hide the truth, or slavery to the lie you choose to believe. But in one way or another, it is bondage.

Reread **Matthew 11:28-30**. Which yoke do you prefer? Is there any area of your life that you have allowed to be corrupted by deception?

_____

Only by living in truth can you truly be free.

day four

God granted Joshua his request to extend the day and guarantee victory for His people. He manipulated the earth, and the *"sun stopped in the middle of the sky and delayed going down about a full day"* (**Joshua 10:13**).

We can get so caught up in our failures, our doubts, our guilt, and our pride that we don't ask God to move on our behalf. He wants you to be victorious in life. He loves you so much He sent His Son, His only Son, so that you would not perish but have eternal life (**John 3:16**). Not only that, but through Christ, God gave you the opportunity to live a life here on earth that is victorious and abundant.

Below, read the KING JAMES VERSION of **John 10:10.**

> *The thief cometh not, but for to steal, and to kill, and to destroy:*
> *I am come that they might have life, and that they might have*
> *it more abundantly.*

Joshua called the Israelites "mighty men of valor" (**Joshua 1:14** KJV). Valor is defined as "courage or bravery."[14] As warriors in the Lord's army, we too are called to courageously seek victory every day of our lives. We are intended to be mighty Christians of valor!

DISCIPLINES OF ENGAGEMENT

Some trust in chariots and some in horses,
but we trust in the name of the Lord our God.

PSALM 20:7

week 6 • day 1

THE HABIT OF OBEDIENCE

week 6 • day 2

SIMPLE VICTORY

week 6 • day 3

REFLECTING VICTORY

week 6 • day 4

PRAISE HIM

week 6 • day 5

PERSONAL APPLICATION

THE HABIT OF OBEDIENCE

The Lord your God commands you this day to follow these decrees and laws;
carefully observe them with all your heart and with all your soul.
Deuteronomy 26:16

After defeating the five armies that attacked Gibeon, the Israelites returned to their camp at Gilgal to rest. The next two lessons will include a good deal of warfare and ugly battles. God has some wonderful things to teach us – even in the ugliness of war.

After returning to Gilgal, Joshua got word that the five kings were hiding in a cave in Makkedah. The Israelites made their way to Makkedah and set up camp.

Read **Joshua 10:16-28**. What did Joshua have the army commanders do to the five kings (**v. 24**)?

_____

_____

_____

_____

Stepping on the neck, an eastern custom of conquerors, is pictured on many Egyptian and Assyrian monuments.[15] It was the ultimate humiliation for a king.

What words did Joshua use to encourage his commanders (**v. 25**)?

_____

_____

_____

_____

Joshua was a great leader because he was a great student. When he was afraid, God used these words to give him courage and firmness of purpose. Joshua didn't just listen to God, he learned from God and tried to put what he learned into practice.

Joshua hanged the kings, then had their bodies thrown into the cave. Once again, he erected a memorial of large rocks as a reminder of the victory the Lord brought in Makkedah.

Update your map by drawing a red line from Gibeon to Makkedah.

Now read **Joshua 10:29-43**.

Draw a red line on your map from Makkedah to Libnah, from Libnah to Lachish, from Lachish to Eglon, from Eglon to Hebron, and from Hebron to Debir.

Compare **Deuteronomy 20:16** to **Joshua 10:40**.

What specific instruction did Joshua follow?

_____

_____

Although he made a few mistakes, Joshua's obvious desire was to live in absolute obedience to his Lord. He made obedience a habit.

Joshua gave God credit for the victories in his life. He didn't call upon the Lord for help, then announce the great things that he had done. He didn't brag about his great strategies. Joshua continually pointed to God as the source of every victory.

Is there someone who has impacted your walk with God by making you aware of the activity of God in his or her life? If so, who?

_____

_____

Have you ever thanked this person or shared how you have been impacted? If not, take a few minutes to write a note of encouragement and thanks.

week 6 · day 2

SIMPLE VICTORY

Some trust in chariots and some in horses,
but we trust in the name of the Lord our God.
Psalm 20:7

The southern cities had been conquered. The next order of business was the north. But the king of Hazor was already taking action. Read **Joshua 11:1-6**.

On your map, locate the cities of Hazor, Dor, and Mizpah and the Sea of Kinnereth. Draw a dotted blue line from each point to outline the areas that the northern kings represented.

What instructions did Joshua receive? **(v. 6)**

_____

_____

_____

_____

Now read **Joshua 11:7-23**. The Israelites were allowed to take valuables and livestock from conquered cities, but Joshua destroyed anyone who breathed, just as the Lord commanded. What else did Joshua make sure to point out? **(v. 19)**

_____

_____

Joshua had been deceived once, but he made sure to document the fact that he didn't make that mistake again. Not one other city was able to manipulate Joshua into making a peace treaty. He had learned his lesson – the hard way.

God told Joshua to "hamstring the horses and burn the chariots." Hamstringing consisted of cutting the tendons in the legs, crippling the animals so that they would be useless in battle. [16] Why do you think God had the Israelites cripple the horses and burn the chariots instead of using them to increase their own productivity in battle?

_____

_____

_____

Perhaps God knew the Israelites would be prone to trust in the horses and chariots rather than trusting in the One who provided them.

Write **Psalm 20:7**.

_____

_____

_____

_____

Often, when we sense God calling us to a task, we begin by implementing the latest program or philosophy. Perhaps we buy the snazziest visual aids and the newest electronic equipment. But sometimes God wants us to use simple methods in order to bring Him greater glory. There is nothing wrong with tools that increase productivity or create excitement, as long as we seek God's guidance before we use them. We should never trust in a program or piece of equipment.

God knew the Israelites would implement their own strategies if they kept those horses and chariots. Joshua listened carefully and carried out God's instructions faithfully.

For several years I was a member of the praise team for Beth Moore Bible Studies. The women on that team were extremely talented singers. But for the first few years, the team led worship by singing along with popular praise and worship CDs. I must admit, when Beth first mentioned the idea I didn't think singing along with artists on a CD would work. But women came back week after week, year after year, excited about worship time. I cannot explain why this simple method of praise and worship worked so effectively except to say that we kept God as the focus. God didn't want us to trust in the voices and musical talents of the women on that team. He wanted us to trust in Him, get together to worship, and lead other women to do the same. God can accomplish more with simplistic methods than we could ever accomplish with the most advanced technology.

Do you sense God prompting you to simplify your approach to anything in your life? If so, explain.

_____

_____

_____

Joshua 11:23 tells us that Joshua took the entire land. Write out the last sentence in **verse 23**.

_____

_____

The word *rest* in this passage is the Hebrew word *shaqat*. It means "repose, idleness, quiet, be at rest, settle, be still." This wasn't an intermission, as discussed last week. This was a chance for the Israelites to settle in and rest. We can almost feel their relief as we read **verse 23**.

We all need rest from the battles of life. Ask God to provide a few quiet moments for you to relax and rest today; then use the time to get away from stresses and struggles to do something relaxing.

week 6 · day 3

REFLECTING VICTORY

Trust in the Lord with all your heart and lean not on your own understanding;
in all your ways acknowledge him, and he will make your paths straight.
Proverbs 3:5-6

We have finished reading about the wars that took place in Canaan. Today, we will review some of the accomplishments of the Israelites. We will also reflect on some symbolism contained in those battles.

Chapter twelve of Joshua defines the areas that were conquered by the Israelites. Glance through it. It will give you a great sense of accomplishment to know you've read an entire book of the Bible at the end of our study.

Chapters five through eleven of Joshua detail the Israelites' journey to the Promised Land. This represents our Christian journey to claim our inheritance in heaven.

In **John 14:2**, what did Jesus say He is doing for you?

_____

_____

_____

_____

There is a place being prepared for you in heaven – our eternal Promised Land. But we can experience a portion of our inheritance here on earth.

I am come that they might have life, and that they might have it more abundantly.
John 10:10 KJV

Through Christ, we can live an abundant, victorious life here on earth in fellowship with our Lord – a taste of heaven. For the remainder of this week, we will reflect on the battles of Joshua and discover principles for living the abundant life God intends for us.

Look back at **Joshua 6:2-5**. At the battle of Jericho, Joshua followed the Lord's instructions carefully even though, from a military standpoint, they didn't make sense. In order to live victoriously, it is imperative that we live in careful obedience to God.

Read **Proverbs 3:5-6**. Joshua didn't lean on his own understanding. He developed the habit of acknowledging and obeying the Lord through all circumstances. Joshua's actions consistently reflected his trust in God. Trust and obedience are interrelated. To faithfully obey the Word of God, we have to trust in His ability to understand and meet our needs.

If you were to evaluate your actions over the last month, what would they reveal about your level of trust in God to meet your needs?

_____

_____

_____

_____

God listens to our requests. Ask Him to meet a specific need that you have right now. Commit to trusting Him to meet that need in His way and in His timing.

Read **Joshua 6:18**. The devoted things had been defiled by the acts of the people living in Jericho and were marked for total destruction.

As review, read **Deuteronomy 13:12-16**.

The entire town was destroyed to protect the Israelites from the effects of a detestable lifestyle. God instructed the Israelites to keep away from the items He knew would tempt them to go astray. The Israelites had a weakness for worshiping idols. (Remember the golden calf incident!) God was protecting them from their weakness by totally eliminating the temptation.

Everyone has weaknesses. Because we've had different experiences, our weaknesses and areas of temptation may be very different. To enjoy the abundant life God intends for us, it is necessary to totally eliminate certain temptations from our lives.

People who have a tendency to drink too much must eliminate that temptation from their lives. If lust is an issue, particularly if one has been promiscuous or has committed adultery, it may even be necessary to avoid television shows or movies that have sexual content. Sound extreme? Not if we are serious about living in victory. Not if we want to enjoy an intimate relationship with our Lord.

We are warriors in the Lord's army. According to **Ephesians 6:12,** our battle against is whom?

_____

_____

_____

_____

We will examine this in depth next week, but our daily battle is against spiritual forces of evil in the heavenly realms. We struggle against a very real enemy who desires that we fail in our attempt to live in obedience to the Word of God. Our weaknesses make us vulnerable, and that enemy will target any area of weakness.

Achan secretly took some of the accursed things from Jericho, even though God had said to destroy them. He fell to temptation. What effect did his disobedience have on the Israelites? (**See Joshua 7.**)

_____

_____

_____

_____

God is holy and will not be in the presence of sin. Without the Lord, the battle of Ai was lost and thirty-six men were killed. Sadly, when we fall to temptation, our sin has an adverse effect on those around us.

Sin has another tragic consequence. Reread **Joshua 6:24-26.**

No one was to rebuild the city of Jericho. What was the cost of rebuilding the city? (**v. 26**)

_____

If we rebuild, or revisit patterns of sin in our lives, our children will be affected.

Read **Exodus 20:4-6.**

Now read a portion of verse 5 from the KING JAMES VERSION:

> _...visiting the iniquity of the fathers upon the children_
> _unto the third and fourth generation of them that hate me..._

God witnesses the effects our sin has on our children to the third and fourth generation. Our children will have a natural tendency to struggle with the same temptations and sins they see us struggle with.

Are there temptations or sins that your parents struggled with that have affected you as an adult? If so, how?

_____

_____

_____

_____

That truth alone should give us incentive to do our best to avoid falling into a pattern of sin. Through Christ we have the power to stop the cycles of sin in our families.

Spend the remainder of the day reflecting on your weaknesses and your strengths. Take them to God in total honesty and ask Him to reveal any changes you need to make. Pray that He will give you the courage to make them.

week 6 · day 4

PRAISE HIM

*Joshua set up the twelve stones that had been in the middle of the Jordan
at the spot where the priests who carried the ark of the covenant had stood.
And they are there to this day.*

Joshua 4:9

Today we will continue our review of the battles in Canaan. Joshua made a conscious effort to give God the glory for his successes. He knew his victories didn't come by his own strength, wisdom, or strategy. Joshua was completely dependent upon God.

Look back at **Joshua 8:18-19, 26.** In **verse 18,** what did the Lord tell Joshua to do?

_____

_____

What happened as he did this (**v. 19**)?

_____

_____

Moses had raised his staff to the Lord in Joshua's first battle. Now Joshua acknowledged God as the victor by raising the javelin toward Ai to testify to his faith. When Joshua raised the javelin toward Ai in acknowledgment of God, the ambushes began.

Let's read about another incident where ambushes were set against the enemy. Read **2 Chronicles 20:1-22.**

What happened when the men began to sing and praise the Lord (**v.22**)?

_____

_____

_____

_____

_____

When Jehoshaphat bowed down and worshiped the Lord, he acknowledged God as victor. The songs of praise were evidence of the people's faith. Is there a battle you are facing right now that you know you can't win on your own?

_____

Praise the Lord in a loud voice! Acknowledge Him and act in faith. He may just send out a heavenly ambush on your behalf. Don't be afraid to ask Him to come to your aid.

Look back at **Joshua 10:12-14**. Joshua asked the Lord to cause the sun to stand still, and God granted his request. What could you possibly ask Him for that would require a miracle like that?

Charles H. Spurgeon said, "O people of God, be great believers! Little faith will bring your souls to Heaven, but great faith will bring Heaven to your souls." Ask God to give you great faith.

Now look back at **Joshua 4:8-9**.

Setting up memorials is an important aspect of living in victory. We are prone to doubt and question when we face trials. Sometimes we begin to believe that we don't really matter to God. We may feel He has abandoned us.

Have you ever felt abandoned by God? If so, describe the circumstances.

_____
_____
_____
_____

Look again at God's words as recorded in **Joshua 1:9**.

God will be with us wherever we go. We need to be reminded of that, just like Joshua. Memorials serve as visual reminders. By remembering God's faithful provision in the past, we are strengthened to believe He will supply our needs again.

As I have already shared, God once used **Psalm 23** to speak to me powerfully during a time of difficulty in my life. That psalm will always remind me of God's faithfulness to lead me through my "dark valley." I have Psalm 23 beautifully printed on a card, which I keep just below my computer screen on my desk. It is a constant reminder of that time when God revealed Himself to me so clearly. It is proof that He loves me – and there are times when I need to be reminded.

What evidence did you find of God's faithfulness through the lessons this week?

_____

_____

_____

_____

He is your Shepherd! As a way of closing, read **Psalm 23** out loud.

week 6 · day 5

PERSONAL APPLICATION

day one

Joshua had cultivated a habit of obedience. How obedient are you on a daily basis? Are you attempting to live your life according to the Word of God? No one is perfect, but are you doing your best every day? On the chart below, plot the frequency of how often you sense a desire to live your life in accordance with God's Word.

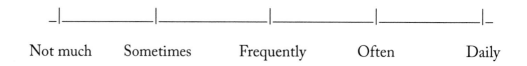

| Not much | Sometimes | Frequently | Often | Daily |

Look back at **Genesis 12:1-5**. Abraham was seventy-five years old when God called him to leave his country, his people, and his father's household. He could have objected. Yet verse four tells us he eventually did what God told him to do, when God told him to do it.

Now read **Genesis 12:6-7**. Because of Abraham's faithful obedience, his descendants inherited the land of Canaan. But more important, through his Seed (our blessed Savior, Jesus) we share the inheritance of eternal life in heaven with our Lord (**Galatians 3:29**).

day two

Joshua defeated the northern kings and conquered their cities. The Israelites hamstrung the horses and burned the chariots, just as the Lord commanded. They experienced victory! Let's review what Joshua did next.

Reread **Joshua 11:21-23**.

The Anakites were the giants we read about earlier in our study. The Israelites feared them. Interestingly, the biggest giant in most of our lives is often fear itself. Joshua understood that in order to truly have "rest from war," he had to rid the land of fear. Likewise, for us to truly find rest for our souls, we must rid our lives of the crippling effects of fear.

What circumstances have caused you the greatest fear recently?

_____

_____

_____

_____

Read **Psalm 20** in its entirety, relating it to your specific fears.

Trust God. He will answer when you call!

> *We will shout for joy when you are victorious*
> *and will lift up our banners in the name of our God.*
> Psalm 20:5

day three

We looked at the destruction of Jericho and asked God to reveal things (temptations) we need to eliminate from our lives in order to escape contamination.

The word *contaminate* is defined as "to spoil the purity of."[17] Sin spoils the purity of our lives. Look up the following verses and note what they tell us about purity:

Matthew 5:8 _____

Philippians 4:8 _____

2 Timothy 2:22 _____

What are some ways we can be polluted by our world?

_____

_____

_____

_____

_____

Ask God for the strength to avoid those things that contaminate your purity.

day four

I have a memorial that hangs by my desk. It is a framed mural drawn by the staff and children of a Montessori preschool that my husband and I helped establish several years ago. Through tragic circumstances, our daughter's previous Montessori school was forced to fold mid-year. The staff had worked together for years. They were loyal employees, gifted teachers, and loving caretakers. They were out of work, and our children, some in kindergarten, were without a school. All of the parents as well as the staff were devastated. By the grace of God, thirteen families pooled what little financial resources we had, located a small building, renovated it into a schoolhouse, and opened the doors of a new Montessori school in a little over two months.

My memorial mural has the names of each of those precious children written delicately along the stem of their chosen flower. Each flower was sponge-painted with a pudgy little hand. That mural reminds me of God's faithfulness to provide a place for those dear children to flourish and bloom in the midst of turmoil and tragedy.

Record at least one time you personally experienced the faithfulness of God.

_____
_____
_____
_____
_____
_____
_____
_____

Take time to set up some memorials of God's faithfulness in your home. If you have children, get them involved. Discuss memorials as a family and set them up together. They will be tremendous faith builders for years to come.

The Israelites conquered the armies in Canaan. They were victorious in battle and were ready to begin enjoying their inheritance.

week 7

SPIRITUAL BOOT CAMP

I tell you this, and insist on it in the Lord, that you must no longer live
as the Gentiles do, in the futility of their thinking.

EPHESIANS 4:17

week 7 • day 1

THE BASICS

week 7 • day 2

A SACRIFICIAL VOW

week 7 • day 3

DECEPTIVE STRATEGIES

week 7 • day 4

THE ACCUSER

week 7 • day 5

THE EXERCISE OF PRAYER

week 7 • day 1

THE BASICS

I tell you this, and insist on it in the Lord,
that you must no longer live as the Gentiles do, in the futility of their thinking.
Ephesians 4:17

Just as the Israelites had to defeat the people in Canaan in order to live successfully in the Promised Land, we also must defeat a very real enemy in order to live the fruitful, abundant life God intends for us. Our battle isn't against people for land, but against a spiritual enemy who wages war against our souls.

Just as soldiers are trained before stepping onto the battlefield, Christians need training before they can be effective warriors in the Lord's army. We will spend the next two weeks in what we'll call "Spiritual Boot Camp." We will study some basics of spiritual warfare presented in the format of military basic training. This portion of our study should enable you to not only visualize yourself as a warrior in the Lord's army, but also to put your training to practical use.

Before attending boot camp, military recruits are tested to see if they meet certain qualifications. Once those qualifications have been met, they sign an enlistment contract. This official contract identifies them as part of their country's military force.

Let's read **Ephesians 1:1-14** to discover what identifies us as members of the body of Christ and warriors in the Lord's army.

When you believed the Gospel of salvation, you became part of the body of Christ. Having believed, you were given the gift of the Holy Spirit, who is the official mark identifying you as a soldier on active duty in God's army. If you are not certain that you are marked with the seal of the Holy Spirit, here are a few scriptures that will help confirm it.

Read **John 3:16**. Do you believe Jesus is the Son of God and that He died for your sins? _____

Now Read **Romans 10:9**. Have you confessed that Jesus is Lord and believed it in your heart? _____

The Holy Spirit is your seal, the mark of a believer, and the guarantee that you are God's possession.

There is one more important step in identifying yourself as a part of the Lord's army. Read **Colossians 2:9-12** to learn what it is.

What do you learn about the importance of baptism from these passages?

_____

_____

Just as circumcision identified the Jews as God's covenant people, baptism publicly identifies us as members of the Lord's army. If you haven't been baptized, contact your pastor or a church leader. Ask whatever questions you need to ask, and publicly identify yourself as part of the body of Christ.

Read and sign the "Enlistment Contract" on the next page of your workbook. After signing it, turn to the next page to begin your training.

ENLISTMENT CONTRACT

I _____ *am a member of the Body of Christ. I have been marked with a seal, the promised Holy Spirit. I ask Him to teach me what it means to put on the full armor of God.*

I commit to completing Spiritual Boot Camp, including all homework.

I sincerely desire to become an effective warrior in the Lord's army so that I can live the abundant, victorious life God intends for me.

_____

Signature

_____

Date

Spiritual Boot Camp
Walking with God

Welcome to Spiritual Boot Camp! At Reception, recruits are issued a basic daily uniform (BDU) and identification tags.[18] They remove the clothes that identified them as civilians and put on the BDUs identifying them with the armed forces. As members of the armed forces, they will take on whole new identities characterized by their disciplined lifestyle.

As believers in Christ, we also take on a new identity that should be distinctive. Read **Ephesians 4:22-24**.

To become the warrior God intends you to be, it is crucial that you put off the old self, which identified you as part of the world. You must put on a new self, which is created to be like God in true righteousness and holiness.

Read **Ephesians 4:25-32**, then make a list of the things we must "put off" and those we must "put on" to make the transition.

PUT OFF	PUT ON
falsehood	truth
anger	Humility (anger rooted in pride)
stealing	generosity / contentment
unwholesome talk	Kind
bitterness	compassionate
rage	Forgiveness
anger	LOVE
brawling	
slander	
malice	Imitate Jesus

Your answers may differ slightly from mine, but these verses make a clear distinction between the Spirit-filled life of a dedicated believer and that of a Christian who is still living like the world. These adjustments in your lifestyle set you apart, like new clothes (BDUs) that you put on to make a transition from a worldly lifestyle to a lifestyle that identifies you as a member of the Lord's army.

The concept of putting off the old and putting on new clothes of righteousness is beautifully portrayed in one of Zechariah's visions.

Read **Zechariah 3:1-9.** (This is not the same Joshua we have been reading about in our study. This Joshua was a high priest.)

Fill in the blanks from **verses 4** and **5:**

"See, I have taken away your __*filthy*__ *, and I will put rich garments on you."* __*clothes*__

Then I said, "Put a __*clean turban*__ *on his head."*

This vision was symbolic of Christ's death on the cross, which "in a single day" (v. 9) removed the sin of all the land. Did you notice that Joshua received new, rich garments?

Members of the armed forces are issued an item to wear around their necks: their dog tags. Engraved on these little metal plates is the most vital information about the person wearing them: that person's identity. As a member of the Lord's army, you should know what God has engraved on your dog tags.

Read **1 Peter 2:9.**

You may be wondering what this has to do with military dog tags. All Christians are part of a royal priesthood. Every one of us is considered a priest with all the privileges. The high priest Joshua received a clean turban for his head. It was customary for priests to wear turbans during Old Testament times. These turbans had an inscription.

Read **Exodus 28:36-38** to see what was engraved on the plate that was on the front of the turban.

__Holy to the Lord__

As a member of the royal priesthood, Jesus is our high priest. He is holy and, through Him we too are considered "Holy to the Lord." As you enter the army of the Lord, your "dog tag" is inscribed with these words. Treasure them, for it is only through Christ that you wear this spiritual identity in the eyes of our God.

No matter what you have done in the past, no matter where you have been, when you became a Christian, you became holy to the Lord. Because you accepted Christ, your offerings are acceptable to God. You have been washed clean. Your filthy clothes have been removed and Christ has placed fresh, rich garments upon you. Whenever your heavenly Father looks at you, He sees you as holy and acceptable.

By now you should have redeemed the coupon you found at the end of week one. Open the package and slip your Spiritual Identification tag around your neck. Then spend a few moments in prayer thanking God for your identification in Christ as HOLY TO THE LORD.

week 7 • day 2

A SACRIFICAL VOW

When a man makes a vow to the Lord or takes an oath to obligate himself by a pledge,
he must not break his word but must do everything he said.
Numbers 30:2

Welcome to Day Two of boot camp. With your BDUs and dog tag issued, we are ready to do the customary "shaving of the head." Not literally. But in the armed forces, once the paperwork is in order, every male soldier's head is shaved. The military wants every individual to lose his or her previous identity and become anonymous.[19] In Spiritual Boot Camp, we also lose our previous identity, but the goal is to be different – transformed into the likeness of Christ – not to become anonymous.

Those God foreknew he also predestined to be conformed to the likeness of his Son.
Romans 8:29

When a soldier has his head shaved, it is an immediate outward indication of the transformation that is taking place on the inside. His bald head continually reminds him of his commitment to become a soldier.

I'm reminded of an Old Testament Nazarite vow of separation that called for letting one's hair grow until the period of separation had been completed. When that period ended, the hair was shaved and burned as an offering to God. Let's read about the vow.

Read **Numbers 6:1-8**.

Who could make this vow (**v. 2**)?

_____

The fact that both men and women could take this vow was extremely unusual. The Nazarite vow was also special because it was made by choice. Its purpose was to allow the individuals to separate, or consecrate, themselves for God's purposes.

The Nazarite vow required the individual to abstain from wine or any fermented drink. In Scripture, wine represents natural joy. This vow to abstain symbolized the Nazarite's desire to find joy from God alone.[20] Long hair was an outward reminder to the individuals of their vow. It was also a sign to others that this person was set apart and consecrated to God. The Apostle Paul once took this vow. Let's examine the circumstances that likely prompted him to do so.

Read **Acts 18:18**.

Paul cut his hair when he had completed his Nazarite vow. You may wonder why Paul would have taken this Old Testament vow. The answer lies with the state of Corinth at the time. The whole city was known for its sinful, immoral, drunken lifestyle. For their religious ideal, the Corinthians had adopted Venus, the goddess of love. A temple built in her honor employed more than 1,000 prostitutes.[21]

Paul knew that to be effective and to remain pure while ministering in Corinth, he needed to be distinctive. He took this vow to protect himself from temptation and to set himself apart from the sinful, shameless lifestyle of the Corinthians.

As we prepare to become effective warriors for Christ, it is imperative that we also consecrate ourselves to God. Are you ready to take a vow of separation to set yourself apart for God's purposes? As indicated in Numbers 6:2, this vow is voluntary. We are going to modify the vow somewhat, but the purpose is the same – to dedicate ourselves to God.

Prayerfully consider entering into a two-week vow of separation to God. Your abstinence does not have to be from wine. You should choose to abstain from something that brings you "natural joy." I suggest giving up something that is part of your daily routine.

For example, I gave up coffee. I love coffee. I drink it every morning and some afternoons. I enjoy it black, with no cream or sugar. I don't drink decaf. So, this is a very sacrificial vow for me. It involves headaches and requires me to get more sleep. (I am very much a Type-A personality and would be perfectly happy if sleeping were not a requirement for survival.) Yes, I gain much "natural joy" from drinking coffee.

Before we continue, let's consider the seriousness of making a vow to God.

Read **Numbers 30:1-2.** When you obligate yourself by a pledge, what must you do?

_____

Read **Ecclesiastes 5:4-7.**

Do not enter into a vow in a flippant manner. Breaking a vow is sin, and God takes it very seriously. Because we have forgiveness for sin through Christ, if you *should* make a vow of separation to God and fail, you can be forgiven.

Read **Matthew 4:1-7.**

If Christ wouldn't put God to the test, we certainly shouldn't either.

Over fifteen years ago I was convicted to abstain from alcohol, not only for a temporary period of time, but for always. At that time I nearly always had at least one glass of wine in the evening. I was not an alcoholic, but alcohol had been a source of many painful, destructive choices since my youth. When I was drinking, my sinful nature would often take over. I realized that in order to live a life worthy of my calling, worthy of the death and sacrifice that Christ had endured for me, I needed to completely eliminate alcohol from my life.

I knew I wasn't strong enough to accomplish this abstinence on my own. I had begun drinking as a teenager, and alcohol was still a big part of my life.

While I was seeking a way to keep the vow to abstain from alcohol, God led me to **Mark 14:22-25:**

> *While they were eating, Jesus took bread, gave thanks and broke it, and gave it to his disciples, saying, "Take it; this is my body." Then he took the cup, gave thanks and offered it to them, and they all drank from it. "This is my blood of the covenant, which is poured out for many," he said to them. "I tell you the truth, I will not drink again of the fruit of the vine until that day when I drink it anew in the kingdom of God."*

I fight back tears when I remember the quickening I felt in my spirit as I read **Mark 14:25.** I knew immediately that God had supplied me with the motivation I needed to take the vow and keep it. I said these words to Jesus, my Lord and my King: "I will not drink again of the fruit of the vine until that day when I drink it with You, anew in the kingdom of God."

I have not had a glass of wine since that time. I still sometimes crave it, but whenever I am tempted I imagine the day that I will drink it in heaven face to face with my Lord. I don't believe I could ever bring myself to break that vow, for it has become for me a sacrificial offering to Christ – a thank offering.

I share this testimony not to draw attention to myself (if anything it reveals my weakness, not my strength) but because I want you to take this exercise seriously. Realize that God might call you to make a vow to give up something that is not beneficial – something that hinders your ability to live a life that is set apart for God. And He may prompt you to give it up permanently, as He did me.

Spend some time in prayer and ask God to reveal something in your life that you need to abstain from. Are you willing to take a two-week vow of abstinence in order to set yourself apart for your God? If so, write what you will abstain from.

_____

_____

I hope you have chosen something that is difficult to give up. During the next two weeks, when you find yourself desiring that which you have given up, draw close to God. Ask Him to fill that void with more of Himself. He is faithful and He will answer your call.

Read **Psalm 20**. We have read it before, but it is one of my favorite Psalms. He will honor your sacrifices and accept your offerings. Rise up and stand firm!

week 7 · day 3

DECEPTIVE STRATEGIES

Stand firm then, with the belt of truth buckled around your waist.
Ephesians 6:14

Today, we will move into Phase One of our basic training. In this phase, you will become familiar with your enemy. For the next two weeks of our study, we will symbolically compare Satan's strategy and tactics to those of a drill instructor. Please understand, this is not a literal comparison. I am in no way suggesting that real military drill instructors are evil. Their purpose during basic training is to break down new recruits in order to make them conform and become effective soldiers.

In the Lord's army, the opposite is required. In order for you to become the warrior God intends, it is necessary that you be built up so that you will not conform to the pattern of the world, but will be transformed by the renewing of your mind.

Read **Romans 12:2**.

Satan's strategy is to break you down and cause you to conform to the pattern of the world. This battle takes place in your mind. His tactics are to confuse and disorient you.

Satan wants you to believe he has total control over your life.

Read **Matthew 10:26-31**.

Even the hairs of your head are numbered. God cares more for you than for the sparrows, yet not one of them falls to the ground apart from His will.

Below, read **Ephesians 6:12** from the KING JAMES VERSION.

*We wrestle not against flesh and blood, but against principalities, against powers, against the **rulers of the darkness** of this world, against spiritual wickedness in high places.* (emphasis added)

Who is the ruler of the darkness? _____

Read **Psalm 18:1-19**.

God is in control. The very earth trembles when He is angry. He will "thunder down from heaven." He will shoot His arrows and scatter the enemy on your behalf. Your God delights in you! He is greater than your enemy. Satan doesn't want you to know that, but it is true.

Satan attempts to control by withholding information.

Every soldier entering combat is issued specially designed protective gear. During an engagement with the enemy, each piece of that gear contributes to the protection, even the survival, of that individual.

Today, let's examine the first listed vital piece of armor God has issued His warriors. Fill in the blanks from **Ephesians 6:13-14**:

> *Put on the full armor of God, so that when the day of evil comes, you may be able to stand your ground, and after you have done everything, to stand. Stand firm then, with the _____ _____ _____ buckled around your waist.*

What exactly is the belt of truth? The term in Greek is *aletheuo*, which means "to be true in doctrine and profession – to speak (tell) the truth." It is a twofold issue. You need to know the truth (God's Word) and you also need to be truthful.

Nothing pleases the enemy more than a believer who does not study the Word of God. Satan knows the Word. If you don't, he will use your lack of knowledge as a means to gain control – a foothold.

The following verses give information about God's Word. Look up each of them and write what truth you learn about the Word of God on the line provided.

Psalm 18:30 _Flawless_____

Psalm 33:4 _right & true_____

Psalm 119:9 _Keeps your way pure_____

Psalm 119:105 _lamp to feet, light to path_____

God's Word is our measuring stick. Tony Evans puts it this way: "The truth is an objective standard that stands outside our experiences and above our opinions. The standard of truth is the Word of God. The belt of truth is becoming more and more important because we live in a world that no longer accepts objective truth."[22]

If we are not spending time every day in the Word of God, we are not keeping ourselves established in truth and we cannot be the warriors God has called us to be. The more fuzzy and skewed our societal standards become, the more important it is for us to be in the truth every day.

In addition to knowing the Word, wearing the belt of truth means we must maintain a standard of honesty. Read **2 Corinthians 4:2**.

We cannot allow ourselves to use deception. Deception, as with the Gibeonites, always leads to bondage of one form or another. In order to live the abundant, victorious life God intends, we must be able to stand our ground when evil comes against us – and it will. The belt of truth protects us against the schemes of our enemy.

What does **Proverbs 12:19** tell you about lies?

_____

Read **Proverbs 20:17**.

Remember the Gibeonites we came across earlier? They tasted the sweetness of victory for a time, but soon their ruse was discovered and they ended up with a mouth full of gravel. A lie may seem easy for a time, but eventually it will be found out. Deception never brings freedom. Secure the belt of truth around your waist and commit yourself to honesty. Then, when the day of evil comes, you will be able to stand your ground.

In 1 **Peter 5:8**, what did Peter compare Satan to?

_____

Your enemy wants you to believe he has control over your life. He wants you to be ignorant of God's Word so he can manipulate you with fear and confusion. Don't give him a foothold.

Finally, my brethren, be strong in the Lord, and in the power of his might.
Ephesians 6:10 KJV

THE ACCUSER

He showed me Joshua the high priest standing before the angel of the Lord,
and Satan standing at his right side to accuse him.
Zechariah 3:1

Yesterday we met our enemy. We discussed some of the deceptive tactics he uses in his attempt to cause fear and confusion. Today, we will see him in his most prominent role – the accuser. As a matter of fact, the word *Satan* comes from a Greek word meaning "to attack or accuse."

Reread **Zechariah 3:1**. Who stood ready to accuse the high priest Joshua?

_____

This is a classic description of Satan's most powerful work. He is the accuser. Nothing gives him more pleasure than humiliating, or shaming, believers. He takes great delight in attempting to convince us that we are unlovable to God and too disgraceful to have a relevant place in the body of Christ.

What were the Lord's words to Satan (**v. 2**)?

_____

The Lord rebuked Satan. This was a severe reprimand, condemning him for his actions.

How does the Lord refer to Joshua in **verse 2**?

_____

This description brought to mind one of my favorite stories in Scripture. The truths contained in these passages were first shared with me by Beth Moore, who mentored me for years through her faithful teaching of God's Word. Once I embraced the principle this story reveals, my life was forever changed.

Daniel, Shadrach, Meshach, and Abednego were Israelites who were taken to Babylon to be slaves for the king. Because Daniel was able to interpret one of the king's dreams, he was promoted to ruler over the entire province of Babylon. He was in charge of all the wise men in the kingdom. At Daniel's request Shadrach, Meshach, and Abednego were appointed as administrators.

Read **Daniel 3:1-27**.

When these three young men refused to serve the king's gods or worship the image of gold he had set up, they were thrown into a blazing furnace. What happened to the soldiers who took Shadrach, Meshach, and Abednego to the fire (**v. 22**)?

_____

How many men were walking, unbound and unharmed, in the fire (**v. 25**)?

_____

What did the king say the fourth man in the fire looked like (**v. 25**)?

_____

Fill in the blanks from verse 27:

> *Shadrach, Meshach and Abednego came out of the fire, and the satraps, prefects, governors and royal advisers crowded around them. They saw that the fire had not harmed their bodies, nor was a hair of their heads singed; their robes were not scorched, and there was _____ _____*
>
> *_____ _____ _____ _____.*

The fire was so hot it killed the strongest soldiers in Nebuchadnezzar's army. Yet when the Son of God walked in that fire with Shadrach, Meshach, and Abednego, not only were they not burned, they came through that fire without even a hint of smoke on them.

When Jesus Christ walks through the fire with you, your filthy clothes are replaced with rich garments, and not a trace of that fire remains.

Satan stands as your accuser. His wants you to believe the scent of your sin will linger on you forever. He wants to convince you that although others can be cleansed and considered HOLY TO THE LORD, you are forever covered in filth.

Write **1 John 1:9**:

_____

_____

_____

_____

When you confess your sins, God is faithful to cleanse you from all unrighteousness. When Satan accuses you, grab your dog tag and cling to the truth that you are HOLY TO THE LORD. You, precious child of God, have been snatched from the fire and you do not have to carry even the scent of your sins. No matter what you have done, you can seek forgiveness and cleansing from the Lord Jesus Christ.

Read **Revelation 20:7-10**.

What is Satan's eternal doom (**v. 10**)?

_____

The devil will not be snatched from the fire. He will be tormented day and night forever and ever. Don't allow him to try to impose his eternal punishment on you.

Does something in your past continually torment you? Do you have difficulty forgiving yourself for something, even though Scripture tells you God has forgiven you? Is there a sin that you have not yet confessed, that you know you need to turn from?

Write it on a separate sheet of paper. Spend as much time in prayer as you need in order to list any sins or mistakes that you need to bring before God and ask His forgiveness. Then put the paper in a blank envelope and seal it. Do not label it or put your name on it. No one will ever see what is written on this paper. It is between you and God.

Keep the envelope tucked in this book until our next session. You will do something special with it.

> *Let us then approach the throne of grace with confidence,*
> *so that we may receive mercy and find grace to help us in our time of need.*
> Hebrews 4:16

137

week 7 · day 5

THE EXERCISE OF PRAYER

He went up on a mountainside by himself to pray.
When evening came, he was there alone.
Matthew 14:23

One of the essential exercises of Spiritual Boot Camp is a daily quiet time with the Lord. We have learned that we are HOLY TO THE LORD, that we are cleansed and purified from sin, and that we have an accuser who would like to convince us otherwise. Unless we are spending consistent time in the presence of our Almighty God, we cannot be the warriors He intends and we will, therefore, live in defeat rather than victory.

In Day One's lesson we discovered that we are part of a royal priesthood and that we have the privileges of a priest. When we come into the presence of the Lord, we experience one of those privileges. Do you remember where the presence of the Lord dwelled in the Tent of Meeting?

_____

(If you need to refresh your memory, reread **Exodus 25:10-22.**)

Read **Exodus 26:30-33.** Where was the ark placed?

_____

The Most Holy Place was separated by a curtain. Only the designated priest could venture behind that curtain, and only at the time specified by God.

Read **Leviticus 16:3-4, 11-14.**

Entering the Most Holy Place behind the curtain was an incredible privilege, and if it was done in an irreverent or improper manner, the priest would die. He was even required to bathe before putting on the sacred garments so he wouldn't defile them.

As I read these passages, it occurred to me how irreverent I can be as I come before God. What about you? Do you find that you sometimes treat God a little too much like a "buddy"? He calls you friend, but He is still God.

Write a prayer of confession.

_____

_____

_____

_____

_____

The numerous preparations the priest made before entering God's presence must have made the anticipation of entering that Most Holy Place overwhelming.

Have you ever taken painstaking effort to prepare for a date with that special someone? The anticipation of spending time together was exciting, and you looked forward to it all day. Perhaps you took a shower or bath. Of course you chose the perfect clothes to wear. You spent extra time making sure your hair was just so. The love you felt for each other made your time together exciting. The sense of adventure increased as you learned more about each other.

As time passes, we become accustomed to that person's presence. We can lose that sense of adventure as we settle into a daily routine. To keep our relationships fresh and alive, it is important to spend time communicating one on one on a regular basis.

The same is true of our relationship with God. To get excited about spending time with Him, we need to continually seek to understand more about Him. No matter how much we learn, there is always more of God for us to experience. There is nothing like receiving a fresh revelation of God or experiencing His grace, His mercy, or His kindness in a whole new way. We can only experience that type of intimacy with our heavenly Father by spending time in His presence and in His Word.

Do you have this kind of relationship with the Lord?

_____

Read **Mark 15:33-39.**

What was torn in two as Jesus "breathed his last" (**v. 38**)?

_____

The curtain that veiled the Most Holy Place was torn in two. Through Christ, we as members of the royal priesthood now have full access to the Most Holy Place where God dwells. Full access! Not just on certain days, not just in certain attire, not only if we were born to the right family. The curtain no longer separates us from the presence of God. We have full access to our heavenly Father through Jesus Christ every moment of our lives. It is a privilege Christ gave His life for.

Do you enter into that Most Holy Place on a regular basis? _____

During difficult times, do you spend more time in prayer, or less? _____

We need to meet with God in a "Most Holy Place" on a regular basis. I strongly suggest keeping a prayer journal to record your time with God. To be honest, this was a struggle for me. I didn't understand the purpose of writing down my prayers (and I certainly didn't want anyone to read them!), so I avoided this method of prayer for years. But I have discovered that recording my prayers forces me to slow down and think them through. I also find it easier to listen to God using this method. But the greatest blessing I have experienced is the ability to look back over my prayers and recognize the activity of God in my life.

By dating each prayer, we leave a trail of our walk with God. We are able to see growth, answered prayer, and the faithful provision of a God who cares deeply about our daily needs.

Your book doesn't have to be fancy or expensive. It can be a spiral-bound notebook or a beautifully bound leather journal. Regardless, it will become a treasure if you use it faithfully. I challenge you to try this method consistently for one month. I feel certain you will find it well worth the effort.

Write your prayers, date them, and bare your soul to your heavenly Father. Record your requests, your fears, and your struggles. When you pray through tears, don't worry if they stain the page. As you faithfully record your prayers, you will become more aware of God's activity in your life.

You may be struggling to establish a consistent prayer time because your schedule is hectic or you don't know how to begin. Start by writing down your daily routine. Divide a piece of paper into seven sections: early morning, late morning, early afternoon, late afternoon, early evening, late evening, overnight.

Write down all of your dedicated time (including when you sleep). Prayerfully examine your schedule and ask God to reveal a good time for you to meet with Him. Establishing a regular prayer time may require a little sacrifice, but the benefits are immeasurable.

If you need some help structuring your prayer time, pick up a Christian devotional. Many of them are set up in daily formats that guide you through prayer. I suggest you also read a Proverb each day. There are thirty-one chapters in Proverbs, which works out to one for each day of the month. When you experience trials, it is helpful to use a concordance to look up verses that address your particular struggle.

Regardless of the method, you will benefit from a daily quiet time. If you're not consistent with one now, commit to begin today. Prayer is crucial to your spiritual health. It is the spiritual discipline that empowers you to effectively utilize all the pieces of your protective gear. It is not an option if you want to live in victory.

PREPARED FOR VICTORY

We demolish arguments and every pretension that sets itself up against the knowledge of God, and we take captive every thought and make it obedient to Christ.

2 CORINTHIANS 10:5

week 8 • day 1

WEAPONS OF DEFENSE

week 8 • day 2

SHINY BOOTS

week 8 • day 3

HELMET OF SALVATION

week 8 • day 4

TAKING YOUR SWORD

week 8 • day 5

ADVANCED TRAINING

WEAPONS OF DEFENSE

You who fear him, trust in the Lord – he is their help and shield.
Psalm 115:11

Last week we focused on our identity in Christ, recognizing our enemy, and some of the tactics Satan uses to defeat us. Today we begin Phase Two of our basic training. In this phase we will learn to effectively use our defensive weapons.

Begin by reading **Ephesians 6:11**.

The armor of God represents several different aspects of our faith that work together to protect our hearts and minds from the attacks of our enemy.

Look again at **Ephesians 6:12**.

The word translated "struggle" can also be translated "wrestle." Wrestling is a one-on-one sport. Our battle against the enemy is a personal one. In order to overcome the strongholds of our opponent, we must wear all of our protective gear. We've already discussed the belt of truth, so let's begin by taking a look at the breastplate of righteousness.

Fill in the blanks from **Ephesians 6:14**.

> *Stand firm then, with the belt of truth buckled around your waist, with the* _____ _____ _____ *in place.*

For the ancient soldier, the breastplate served the same purpose as our modern body armor. Think of the breastplate as a protective covering of Christ's righteousness. The Greek word *dikaiosune*, translated as "righteousness" in this verse, means "equity of character or act; justification, righteousness."

What does equity of character mean to you?

_____

_____

_____

_____

The breastplate of righteousness is not your own righteousness, but Christ's. In essence, Christ made a deposit of His righteousness into your character account. It is His righteousness that allows you to have a more holy character. You have equity of character through Christ.

Satan is our accuser. He wants us to believe we are forever tainted by our sinful, unrighteous behavior. The breastplate of righteousness (Christ's character) protects our hearts from this lie. It is Christ's righteous identity transferred to you. You are worthy to wear it because Christ gave it to you as a gift. Your dog tag represents this piece of armor.

We can't just wake up in the morning and decide to try to be righteous. That can easily turn to self-righteousness. Instead, we need to pray for Christ's righteousness to be reflected in all we do.

The WWJD (What would Jesus do?) bracelets so popular at one time are still a wonderful example of a visual reminder to wear your breastplate. By continually asking yourself this question, you are consciously putting on the breastplate of righteousness. When you make a mistake, confess it, and ask God to help you do better next time.

Describe the belt of truth and the breastplate of righteousness in your own words.

Belt of Truth:

_____

_____

_____

_____

Breastplate of Righteousness:

_____

_____

_____

_____

These two pieces of armor work together. You cannot reflect the righteousness of Christ unless you measure your actions against the truth of God's Word, as Christ did.

Do you sense any change you need to make in order for you to reflect more of Christ's righteous character?

_____

_____

_____

_____

Why not do it today?

Now, let's discuss your shield of faith.

According to **Ephesians 6:16,** what is the purpose of the shield of faith?

_____

_____

_____

_____

_____

_____

Roman soldiers carried large shields that were either oval or rectangular and as large as doors.[23] These shields were usually made of wood covered with leather. They were large enough to cover part of the body of the soldier fighting next to the shield holder. Roman soldiers lined up side by side in close formation, with their overlapping shields forming an impenetrable wall covering all of them as they advanced.[24]

Everyone has struggles. When we waver in our faith, we might need to seek the protection of another's shield until we find the strength to carry our own again.

Can you remember a time when another believer picked you up and encouraged you until you were strong enough to carry your own shield again? If so, briefly describe the circumstances.

_____

_____

_____

A Roman soldier could only be partially covered by someone else's shield. No one else's faith can effectively replace our own. We can lean on someone else for a season, but to be the warriors God intends, and live in victory, we must each carry our own shield.

Ephesians 6:16 says, "Take up your shield of faith."

The Hebrew word for "take up" in this verse is *analambano*. It is derived from a word that implies repetition. So we are to repeatedly take up our shields of faith. To live in victory, we must continually take up our shield, not just when we feel like it, or when things are going well, but every day.

Read **Hebrews 11:1, 6.**

Without faith it is impossible to please God, because it is our faith that propels us to action. We can know volumes of Scripture, but knowledge is not faith. Faith is acting on what we say we believe.

According to **Numbers 14:10-11**, what was it that upset God when the Israelites were too afraid to fight for the Promised Land? _____

_____

They refused to act because they didn't trust God to deliver them safely to the Promised Land. They refused to pick up their shields!

Earlier in our study I shared the story of Joe, who experienced great fear and doubt about running his business after the death of his father. At that point in his life, Joe was unable to carry his shield of faith by himself. He sought out a business partner whom he thought would bring him strength. But partnering with the man would have only brought difficulties and debt to his business.

A few years later, I received a phone call from Joe. He had grown strong enough to take up his shield and carry on in business, trusting in the Lord rather than men. The results? His company made the *Houston Chronicle* and the *Houston Business Journal's* list of the top 100 fastest-growing small businesses in Houston for the year 2000.

This is what can happen when we stop relying on others and place our trust in God. When we pick up our shields and advance against our enemy, we defeat the arrows of doubt and despair. Then we will begin to experience victory.

Describe the shield of faith in your own words. _____

_____

_____

_____

Ask God for the courage to take it up every day.

week 8 · day 2

SHINY BOOTS

With your feet fitted with the readiness that comes from the gospel of peace.
Ephesians 6:15

In Christ's time, soldiers wore military sandals. Today they wear combat boots. Part of our protective gear is what I'll call Gospel boots. These boots may hurt your feet for the first several days. This is normal. Your feet must adjust to the protective boot. Expect to develop a few minor blisters.[25]

Let's examine what makes these boots protective. In **Ephesians 6:15**, the word translated "peace" is the Greek word *eirene*. It is derived from the primary verb *eiro*, which means "to join." This verse refers to peace with God, the peace that joins us with Him in blessed reconciliation.

So what does verse 15 mean by "feet fitted with the readiness"? It means that because we know the truth of the Gospel and are reconciled with God, our feet are stable beneath us.

Reread **Ephesians 6:11 and 13** below.

> *Put on the full armor of God so that you can **take your stand** against the devil's schemes…Therefore put on the full armor of God, so that when the day of evil comes, you may **be able to stand** your ground, and after you have done everything, **to stand**.* (emphasis added)

We put on our Gospel combat boots by continually reconciling ourselves with God. Our peace with God enables us to stand our ground against our enemy.

According to **Colossians 1:21-23** what alienates us from God?

_____

The KING JAMES VERSION calls sinful behavior our "wicked works." Our sin alienates us from God. We remain at peace with God by continually confessing our sins and reconciling ourselves to Him.

Openly confessing our sin on a regular basis is not comfortable at first. This is where the blisters come in! But as we do so on a regular basis, we will become more at peace with God, and we will begin to live with the peace of God. The armor is peace with God, but its fruit is an inner peace that defies our understanding.

When I was pregnant with my daughter, Brianna, I had a picture-perfect pregnancy. I felt good and was extremely active. When I began feeling contractions, I went to the hospital and the doctor monitored the fetus's activity. Several nurses came in to check the monitor readings and I began to sense that something was wrong. Yet I remained calm. I knew God's hand was on my pregnancy. My husband and I had not planned to have any more children after our son was born. When I found out I was pregnant, God made it clear that this was His will and He had a purpose for this child.

The doctor told me her heart rate was falling and he suspected the umbilical cord was wrapped around her neck. He wanted to do an immediate C-section. I sensed God's presence and trusted that He was in control. I calmly told the doctor to do it, and off we went to the operating room.

At my first follow-up appointment, my doctor told me how taken aback he was by my reaction when he told me the cord was around Brianna's neck, "Most women would have panicked and gotten very upset." He had seen the peace of God in me that day. He didn't quite understand it, but it impacted him to the point that two weeks later it was still on his mind.

Can you remember a time when you felt the peace of God when your circumstances warranted anything but peace?

_____

_____

_____

_____

There is nothing like being at peace with God and experiencing the peace of God in difficult situations. Our peace is a protective covering that non-believers will long to understand.

There is another purpose for those Gospel combat boots – sharing the Good News with others. Once you break in your boots and get comfortable with daily confession, others will begin to notice a difference in you.

In the military, shining boots are very important. The shinier, the better. They should have at least a minor shine at all times.[26] What is the wax that Christians use to shine our Gospel boots? Love.

What are the greatest commandments (**Mark 12:29-31**)?

_____

_____

Because of our love for God, we make the effort to be at peace with God. When we pour out that love on others, we draw them to God as well. When people notice your shiny boots, ask God for the courage to share the Gospel with them.

Read **Romans 6:23**.

When you share this message while making your life "shine with love," the message sticks. Most of us have been exposed to people who believe the best way to draw lost souls to Christ is by theologically dangling them over the pits of hell. While that may cause some to repent, in my experience it seldom draws them into a love relationship with the Lord. Pour on plenty of love and let them know about the Gift of God. That is what will draw them to Christ.

In conclusion, define "Gospel boots" in your own words:

_____

_____

_____

_____

Let your boots shine!

HELMET OF SALVATION

Therefore if anyone is in Christ, he is a new creation;
the old has gone, the new has come!
2 Corinthians 5:17

In today's lesson we will study the helmet of salvation. Our helmet protects our mind, the control center for our entire body. It is a critical piece of armor because if the enemy can injure our minds, he can hinder our effectiveness in battle.

The Roman helmet consisted of a leather cap with an elaborately decorated crest (bronze covering). It had two cheek pieces and a hinged visor.[27] We will get a better grasp on the concept of our helmet as it relates to spiritual warfare by looking at the cap and the crest individually.

The leather cap was worn under the crest of the helmet. It provided protection for the brain because it absorbed some of the impact from any blow received to the head. The leather cap has a deeper meaning when it comes to spiritual warfare.

According to **Genesis 3:21**, what did the Lord clothe Adam and Eve with after they sinned by eating the forbidden fruit in the Garden of Eden?

_____

God covered their shame with animal skin. Leather is animal skin that has been treated and tanned. The leather cap represents our protection from Satan's most powerful arrow – shame. Webster's defines shame as "a painful sense of guilt or inadequacy."[28] Causing Christians to feel guilt and shame is Satan's favorite strategy.

Can you recall an event that caused you to feel a painful sense of guilt or inadequacy? If so, I guarantee you that Satan was somehow involved in the situation.

Events that cause us shame are almost always extremely personal, so we won't write this answer down. Instead, spend a few minutes in prayer. Ask God how those feelings have negatively affected your ability to use your gifts and talents to build up His kingdom. Write down what God reveals to you.

_____

_____

_____

_____

_____

_____

_____

What you have written is called a stronghold. It is a situation in which Satan has gained control over your actions by manipulating your thoughts. Strongholds always begin in the mind and are usually related to a painful sense of guilt or inadequacy. Tomorrow, we will talk more about strongholds and learn how to use our swords to overcome them. For now, focus on the fact that strongholds begin in the mind.

The crest of the helmet (pictured below) fit over the leather cap. Soldiers often scratched the names of their centurions onto their helmets as a mark of ownership.[29] We learned in Week Three that Jesus Christ is the Commander of the Lord's army. Your helmet, fittingly referred to as the helmet of salvation, is marked with the name of your Savior. Write His name on the crest pictured here.

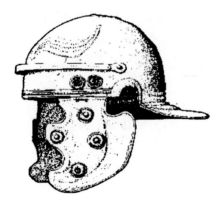

Your helmet is the assurance that you belong to Christ, that your sins are forgiven, and that you no longer carry the scent of sin – shame.

Read **2 Corinthians 5:16-21**.

When you accepted Christ as your Lord and Savior, you became a new creation who has the opportunity for eternal fellowship with God.

If you believe in Jesus Christ, you can feel secure in your salvation. Your sins are covered and you no longer have to carry the heavy and painful burden of shame. The assurance of salvation and forgiveness through Christ is the helmet that protects your mind from the lies of the enemy.

Read **Ephesians 2:4-10**.

You have been saved by grace. Nothing can separate you from the love of God in Christ Jesus (**Romans 8:39**), and nothing you can do will earn your salvation. It is a gift from the merciful hand of a loving Father who knit you together in your mother's womb (**Psalm 139:13**).

Do you try to earn your salvation or God's love? If so, how?

_____

_____

_____

_____

God loves you, and has been preparing his kingdom for you since the creation of the world (**Matthew 25:34**). By putting on the helmet of salvation daily, you live with the constant security of knowing you belong to Christ and your sins are forgiven. You do not have to carry the scent of sin.

According to **2 Corinthians 2:15**, what do we smell like to God?

_____

Describe the helmet of salvation in your own words.

_____

_____

Tomorrow we will focus on our swords. There will be some extra work involved in the lesson so allow a little extra time.

week 8 · day 4

TAKING YOUR SWORD

We demolish arguments and every pretension that sets itself up against the knowledge
of God, and we take captive every thought to make it obedient to Christ.
2 Corinthians 10:5

Today we begin Phase Three of Spiritual Boot Camp. Our focus in this lesson is on the sword of the Spirit (God's Word) – the only offensive weapon included in our armor. Our spiritual battlefield is the mind. In order to be victorious, we must learn to defend it. We do this by using our sword (God's Word) to tear down the lies of our enemy and replace them with truth.

Read **2 Corinthians 10:5**.

What does "taking every thought captive to make it obedient to Christ" mean to you?

_____

_____

_____

_____

According to John 1:1 and 1:14, who is the Word of God?_____

We are to take every thought that does not agree with the Word of God and immediately replace it with a thought that does. For instance, let's say you are aware of a need for greeters at your church on Sunday mornings. You really enjoy people and sense that God wants you to help meet this need. You volunteer and are ready to go. But as Sunday morning approaches you begin to think, "What am I doing? I don't know very many people and I don't know what to say. I am going to make a fool out of myself!"

You need to recognize that this argument sets itself up against the Word of God. To yourself, or out loud if necessary, say, "No, I can do all things through Christ who strengthens me" (**Philippians 4:13**). "I trust in the Lord; He is my help and my shield" (**Psalm 115:11**). "God is able to make all grace abound to me so that I have all I need to abound in every good work" (**2 Corinthians. 9:8**). You will feel better just saying those faith-filled words.

But to do this, you must know the Word. Memorizing Scripture comes easier for some than it does for others. But if you gain nothing else from this study, I pray that you will begin to take control of your thoughts through the memorization and personalization of God's Word.

I became a Christian when I was twenty-six years old. My lifestyle had been anything but holy. My self-image was such that I truly believed my son was better off spending ten to twelve hours a day in daycare than with me. My marriage was falling apart. I grew up with tremendous insecurities and had difficulty controlling my temper. I was angry at the world, and my husband received a good amount of my wrath. My only sense of self-worth came from work, so I would step on anyone to climb to the next level of achievement. I hated the person that I was. My life was crumbling around me. I sought the Lord out of absolute desperation.

God changed my life so completely that it is hard for me to believe the person I just wrote about really existed. I have a long way to go, but God has transformed my thinking through the healing truth of His Word.

Read **Romans 12:2.**

Do you believe you can be transformed by the renewing of your mind?_____

Because I had absolutely no knowledge of Scripture, and I knew I needed to change, I began soaking up God's healing Word like a sponge. As I came across a Scripture that meant something to me, I would write it down on an index card and carry it around in my pocket. I remember standing in my office reciting verses, trying desperately to believe what they said. I wanted to believe God loved me and that I was a new creation in Christ. I flooded my mind with truth. Without realizing what I was doing, I began to change my thought processes from that of the world to that of my Savior.

As I began to believe that I was truly forgiven, I was able to forgive others and let go of the bitterness that was eating away at my soul. The anger that once consumed me slowly fell away, layer by painful layer. As God chiseled away my hard exterior with His Word, more and more of my bruised and broken heart was exposed. With time, my anger turned to grief. Eventually, that grief turned to joy!

For about six months, I recited **Psalm 1:1-3** out loud every morning and personalized it. (See below.)

> *I walk not in the counsel of the ungodly, nor stand in the way of sinners, nor sit in the seat of mockers. But my delight is in the law of the Lord; and on that law I meditate day and night. I am like a tree planted by the streams of water, that yields its fruit in season; my leaf does not wither; and whatever I do prospers.*

Look up Psalm 1 in your Bible. What are the first four words?

_____

I recited those verses because God said I would be blessed if I lived in that manner. It was my desire to be blessed by God in every area of my life. I made a conscious effort to live out those verses. I delighted in God's Word. As I saw His righteous character, I found a God who was faithful and worthy of my trust.

This was a slow process, but more than fifteen years later, I can honestly say I am free from the shame and anger that once gripped me so tightly. I still feel sadness when I think back on my life prior to Christ, but the emotion is regret, not shame.

If you are serious about living in victory, you must learn to replace the lies of your enemy with the truth of God's Word. The only way I have found to do that is to memorize and personalize Scripture.

Do you struggle with shame, anger, or bouts of depression? If so, ask God to transform you through the renewing of your mind. Ask Him to heal you with His Word and allow you the joy of sharing a testimony of victory with others. Ask Him to allow you the privilege of bringing Him glory by overcoming strongholds with the truth of His Word.

Yesterday I asked you to identify an experience that caused you to feel inadequate or guilty, and write down how those feelings have affected your ability to use your talents and gifts for God's kingdom. Review your answer, and circle the category below that best describes the thought process that is holding you back.

FEAR   DOUBT   GUILT   LACK OF TRUST

In a concordance or the subject guide in your Bible, look up the word you circled. Look up the verses indicated. If another subject is referenced, look up the verses listed under that subject as well. Look up the remedy for the word you circled (Fear & Doubt = Faith; Guilt = Forgiveness & Justification; Lack of Trust = Trust & Faith).

Keep searching until you find four verses that really encourage you. Write them on index cards. Carry the cards in your pocket every day over the next two weeks and memorize the verses. Pull the cards out while ironing, doing dishes, waiting for an appointment, anytime you can study them. When you are driving, try reciting them without looking. Recite each of them once just before going to sleep and again first thing in the morning.

When thoughts enter your mind that feed your feelings of inadequacy or guilt, immediately say, "No" and recite one of the verses you have chosen. Take the negative thoughts captive and refuse to let them take root. God will transform you by the renewing of your mind.

Keep your index cards for the next session. Have some extra cards on which to write other Scriptures that will be helpful to you.

This process can seem a little overwhelming at first, but avoid the temptation to skip it. If you are having trouble memorizing Scripture from one Bible version, try another one. I love the KING JAMES VERSION because it sounds poetic and I find the verses easier to memorize. Keep searching until you find a version that works for you. You cannot effectively battle your enemy without using your sword.

You can use this method regardless of the stronghold you are dealing with. Focus on one at a time. Keep a healthy supply of index cards. You may wish to file them by category as time goes by.

Write **Ephesians 2:10.**

_____

_____

_____

_____

God has good works for you to do, but you must trust Him enough to allow Him to accomplish that work through you. Your enemy wants to debilitate you by convincing you that you are not a worthy vessel. He will use every circumstance, every secret, and every painful memory to try to convince you of your unworthiness. Take up your sword, and demolish arguments and pretensions (imaginary obstacles) that set themselves up against the knowledge of God (the truth of His Word). Your weapon is available. It may be a bit dusty, but wipe it off and fight. The reward will be a transformation that you never believed possible.

I thank my God every time I remember you. In all my prayers for all of you, I always pray with joy because of your partnership in the gospel from the first day until now, being confident of this, that he who began a good work in you will carry it on to completion until the day of Christ Jesus.
Philippians. 1:3-6

Spend a moment praising God that He will complete His work in you.

week 8 · day 5

ADVANCED TRAINING

Unto the upright there ariseth light in the darkness.
Psalm 112:4 KJV

Today is our final lesson before returning to the book of Joshua. We have become familiar with our BDU (basic daily uniform) and have learned how to utilize each piece of our armor. Now we are ready for some advanced training.

Before getting into the lesson, how are you doing with your vow? Describe your greatest struggle in keeping it.

_____

_____

_____

_____

Is there anything you have learned about yourself or about God through making this vow?

_____

_____

_____

_____

Hang in there; you only have a few days left! Now, let's get on with our training.

Let's begin with the "low crawl." This involves dragging oneself across the ground as low as possible, facedown. This movement is very useful in combat situations.[30] Let's look to Joshua for examples of situations in which this maneuver should be employed during spiritual warfare.

Look back at **Joshua 5:13-15**.

Joshua, realizing he was in the presence of the Lord, "fell facedown to the ground in reverence." What question did Joshua ask after doing so?

_____

_____

Joshua was seeking to hear the Lord's message, and his posture was one of total submission. He was completely submitted to God's will, ready to obey any instruction.

Now look at **Joshua 7:1-6.**

Joshua was compelled by grief, fear, and confusion to fall "facedown" before the Lord. The position indicated total submission. He was seeking God's guidance. But Joshua grieved over his circumstances and desired to fully understand why the event had taken place.

In our most painful and confusing situations, this is exactly the position we should take before the Lord. To get on our faces in prayer before God, we must be willing to totally submit to His will. Unfortunately, we don't often get to the point of complete submission until we are either in a situation that is completely out of our control, or we have messed things up so badly trying to force our will that we have no choice but to submit to His.

Have you ever fallen facedown before the Lord? If so, what circumstances moved you to this position?

_____

_____

_____

_____

If not, give it a try. To live in victory, we need to practice this maneuver until we become experts at it.

We will conclude our Spiritual Boot Camp with a lesson in what we'll call night warfare. During nighttime drills, the bullets of our enemy glow and look like they are just inches away, but this is an illusion.[31] Keeping our perspective during dark periods of our lives, especially at night, is very difficult. Night warfare can be terrifying if we aren't prepared.

This is not a new concept. Think about every suspense thriller you have watched. If you're like me, the ones that impacted you most were those where the enemy attacked at night.

Several years ago a young man I knew was diagnosed with Multiple Sclerosis. He was in his twenties with a wife and a young son. After receiving the diagnosis he was overcome with depression and anxiety. His sleep patterns became sporadic until he was unable to sleep at night. Because his body wasn't strong enough to withstand exhaustion on top of his disease, he became unable to work. According to his wife, the doctors found no medical reason for the elevated symptoms he was experiencing. His depression continued to increase until he was completely disabled, not as much from his disease as from the hopelessness that consumed him. Eventually, his marriage was destroyed. Fatigue and hopelessness caused this once humorous, fun-loving young man to become bitter and hateful. The transformation that took place in this man is a tragic example of night warfare.

Sleep deprivation is one of the tools Satan uses to gain control over our thoughts. Fatigue increases feelings of frustration and irritability. Often, at night we feel alone because the distractions of the day are gone. We are separated from friends and family. It is then that the prince of darkness makes his strongest attacks on our faith. He will use those times when we are most vulnerable to lure us into darkness.

It is in the dark times of life that we discover the depth of our relationship with the Lord. Do we trust Him even when we can't see any evidence of His presence? Do we know He is there even when the silence muffles His voice? In the darkness we will draw on the scriptures that we have memorized. Having Scripture cards is not enough. By memorizing Scripture, the truths contained in God's Word seep into our thought processes and enable us to hang on, even when everything around us seems hopeless.

Read **Psalm 126:5-6**.

The Hebrew word translated "sow" in verse 5 is *zara*. It means, figuratively, to disseminate or plant seed. When you sow (plant the seeds of God's Word in your mind) in tears, you will reap with songs of joy!

Cling to the Word of God with every ounce of strength you can muster. When Satan lures you into the darkness, allow the Word to be your lamp. When you are so overwhelmed with despair that you don't know what to pray, begin to speak the Word with emphasis and determination. You will be feeding your faith and starving your fear with the power that is in the Word. Even if at that moment you don't believe what it says, say it anyway. Eventually, you will come to believe it!

Read **Psalm 119:105**.

Let Him guide you through the darkness.

> *Unto the upright there ariseth light in the darkness.*
> Psalm 112:4 KJV

This concludes Spiritual Boot Camp. My prayer is that you have a better grasp on your righteous identity in Christ and how to put on the full armor of God.

So, what are we fighting for? We are fighting for our inheritance, just as the Israelites were. We are saved by grace, so we are not talking about heaven – that was decided at the Cross. Heaven is our ultimate Promised Land and our eternal home. But we can experience a taste of heaven here on earth when we find our calling.

God created you alone to do something specific here on earth to build His kingdom. If you allow your enemy to hold you back, not only will you miss out, but the entire body of Christ will miss out, as well. Others will have their faith increased when they see you do something that they know you couldn't accomplish on your own. When you step out in faith and allow God to accomplish His work through you, God will get the glory. You are God's precious masterpiece and you were put on this earth for a divine purpose.

As we return to the book of Joshua, we see the Israelites will finally receive their inheritance. God had a specific place for each tribe to live and work the land.

You also have a specific work prepared for you in advance, a ministry. Are you willing to fight for it? Read **2 Corinthians 6:3-7**.

Chances are, none of us will be called to fight for our ministry to the extent that Paul fought for his. But take up your sword in your right hand and your shield in your left, put on your breastplate of righteousness and your helmet of salvation, buckle truth around your waist, and stand firm in the Gospel of peace. Be strong and courageous like Joshua. Do not be terrified; do not be discouraged, for the Lord your God will be with you wherever you go (**Joshua 1:9**).

Now you are prepared for your next duty assignment.

We pick up this week with the thirteenth chapter of Joshua. The Israelites had successfully conquered the Canaanites and enjoyed a long-awaited season of rest. Yet Joshua had not completed his assignment.

THE PROMISED LAND

You also were included in Christ when you heard the word of truth,
the gospel of your salvation. Having believed, you were marked
in him with a seal, the promised Holy Spirit.

EPHESIANS 1:13

week 9 • day 1

A LESSER INHERITANCE

week 9 • day 2

THE LARGEST LOTS

week 9 • day 3

DWELLING PLACE REVEALED

week 9 • day 4

ALLOTTED PORTIONS

week 9 • day 5

PERSONAL APPLICATION

A LESSER INHERITANCE

*This is the inheritance Moses had given when he was in
the plains of Moab across the Jordan east of Jericho.*
Joshua 13:32

Look back at **Deuteronomy 31:7.**

As Joshua walked with God, he led the Israelites to victory. What was Joshua
instructed to do after crossing over into the Promised Land?

_____

_____

Our text this week reads like a real estate deed at times, but try to resist the
temptation to skip some of the reading. I suggest keeping your map handy as we
identify the allotment for each tribe. By coloring and labeling areas on your map,
you will understand the meaning of the material better.

Read **Joshua 13:1-7.**

Parts of the land were still to be conquered, yet what did God tell Joshua to be
sure to do (**v. 6**)?

_____

_____

The land west of the Jordan, conquered and unconquered, was to be divided
among nine and a half tribes. The tribes of Rueben, Gad, and half of the tribe of
Manasseh had requested the land on the east side of the Jordan. Our next text
begins with the allotment of that land.

Read **Joshua 13:8-14.**

Verse 14 reminds us that the Levites did not receive land as their inheritance.
God Himself was their inheritance, and God designated towns within the
territories of each tribe for the Levites. To claim the land east of the Jordan, the
Reubenites, Gadites, and half the tribe of Manasseh had to meet a condition.

Look back at **Numbers 32:20-22**. What was that condition?

_____

_____

_____

_____

Now the tribes had fulfilled their commitment, and the time had finally arrived for their reward.

Read **Joshua 13:15-23**. On your map, locate Medeba, Heshbon and Dibon on the east side of the Jordan. Label the section of land containing these cities Reuben and color it dark green. This land was allotted to the tribe of Reuben.

Now read **Joshua 13:24-28**. Locate Jazer, Ramoth, Mahanaim, and Succoth on your map, also on the east side of the Jordan River. Notice that this area extended all the way to the tip of the Sea of Kinnereth. Label the section of land containing these cities Gad and color it light blue. This land was allotted to the tribe of Gad.

Read **Joshua 13:29-31**. Locate the cities of Ashtaroth and Edrei on your map. Label this section of land East Manasseh and color it dark orange. This land was allotted to half of the tribe of Manasseh.

Read **Joshua 13:32-33**. The Reubenites, Gadites and the half tribe of Manasseh had requested this land to be their inheritance.

Look back at **Numbers 32:1-5**. What reason did these tribes give Moses for desiring this land?

_____

_____

_____

_____

These tribes took what they could see at the time and forfeited the true, yet unseen inheritance that God had for them on the other side of the Jordan. They lacked the faith to believe that God had planned something better for them.

Look at **Joshua 13** verses **15, 24,** and **29**. Who gave the land to these tribes?

_____

In contrast, look at the wording in **Joshua 15:20, 16:4, 18:28,** and **19:1.**

The land to the east of the Jordan was not truly the Israelites' inheritance. These territories had no natural boundaries to the east and were therefore constantly exposed to invasion by the Moabites, Amalekites, and others.[32] This land proved to be less than God desired for His people.

Many times, in order for us to experience all that God has for us, He will require us to give up what appears to be "suitable" or comfortable. Pray that you never allow yourself to settle for what you can see instead of seeking God's best.

Are there any comfortable things that you would have difficulty giving up if you truly believed God was calling you to go elsewhere or do something new? If so, list them.

_____

Ask the Lord to help you let go of anything you cling to other than Him. May He give us the wisdom, patience, and faith to wait for His best.

> *They that wait upon the Lord shall renew their strength;*
> *they shall mount up with wings as eagles;*
> *they shall run, and not be weary; and they shall walk, and not faint.*
> Isaiah 40:31 KJV

week 9 • day 2

THE LARGEST LOTS

The Israelites divided the land, just as the Lord had commanded Moses.
Joshua 14:5

The land east of the Jordan was divided; then came the task of awarding the remaining tribes their inheritance west of the Jordan. Before we begin reading, let's look back at the Lord's commands regarding this process.

Read **Numbers 26:52-56**.

This land was to be divided by lot and by tribal numbers.

Read **Joshua 14:1-9**.

Caleb had maintained his trust in God when God's people refused to go up and take the Promised Land. He had been convinced they "could certainly do it!" He hadn't discounted the fact that the people of Canaan were large, but he knew God was more powerful than any army. Caleb had revealed his faith and trust in Almighty God.

Read the Lord's words regarding Caleb recorded in **Deuteronomy 1:35-36**. Caleb passionately desired to follow God's instructions and sought Him with his whole heart. According to **Psalm 119:2** what is the result of living your life in this manner?

_____

God blessed Caleb with the land he had explored just as He said He would. Let's see how Caleb was presented with his inheritance. Read **Joshua 14:10-15**.

The Hebrew word for Hebron is *Chebrown*. It means "seat of association." Hebron was formerly known as Kiriath Abra; but after Caleb claimed the city, the name was changed.

Based on all that we have studied about him, who do you think the Israelites would have associated Caleb with? _____

_____

Whenever someone referred to Caleb's home, they were reminded that he was placed in the blessed seat of association with his mighty and powerful God.

Look back at **Numbers 34:19.** What tribe was Caleb from?_____

The land was distributed by lot, then by size. Many factors were probably considered in determining the most desirable land and the portion allotted to each tribe. The first lot fell with the tribe of Judah.

Read **Joshua 15:1-4, and 12-20.**

Locate the Desert of Zin, the Sea of Salt, the Wadi River of Egypt, and the Great Sea on your map. These were the boundaries for land allotted to Judah. Label the section of land outlined by these boundaries JUDAH and color it light green. (Be careful when coloring. Another tribe received inheritance within this territory too.) This was the inheritance of the tribe of Judah. Judah, the largest of all of the tribes, received the largest allotment of land.

Read **Joshua 16:1-3.**

While casting lots, the tribes of Ephraim and Manasseh were considered one tribe, Joseph. The tribes were separated as they received separate inheritances.

Now read the remainder of **Joshua chapter 16.**

Locate the city of Shiloh on your map. Label this section of land EPHRAIM and color it red. This was the inheritance of the tribe of Ephraim. Notice not all of the Canaanites were dislodged from the land.

Let's look again at the consequences of failing to completely eliminate the Canaanites from the Promised Land. Read **Deuteronomy 20:17-18** and **31:15-22.**

The Israelites could have carried out God's instructions if they had truly wanted to. God doesn't give us tasks without also equipping us to accomplish them.

Disobedience always brings consequences. Read **Psalm 106:34-43.**

Has God brought to mind any acts of disobedience on your part? If so, write about them on the lines below. (You can write in code if you like.)

_____

_____

_____

_____

_____

_____

Spend a few minutes in prayer and ask God for forgiveness. Make a fresh commitment to obey His commands to the best of your ability.

DWELLING PLACE REVEALED

You are to seek the place the Lord your God will choose from among all your tribes to put his Name there for his dwelling. To that place you must go.
Deuteronomy 12:5

Today we will continue to study the distribution of the Israelites' inheritance. We pick up with the allotment to the tribe of Manasseh, Joseph's firstborn. Ephraim received his inheritance first because Ephraim had been given the blessing of the firstborn by his grandfather Jacob.

Read **Joshua 17:1-4** for some interesting information about some of the descendants of Manasseh.

Let's look at the circumstances that led to these women making their appeal to Joshua and the tribal leaders. Read **Numbers 27:1-7**.

These women followed the Lord's instructions, which protected their father's inheritance from going to another tribe. This story helps us understand that all of God's children, men and women alike, are heirs to His promises. It is particularly notable because at this time most societies regarded women as property, with little or no rights or entitlement.

How does the fact that women as well as men are heirs to God's promises affect you personally?

_____

_____

_____

Read **Galatians 3:26-29**.

We are all one in Christ Jesus!

Now read **Joshua 17:5-13**.

Locate the cities of Shechem, Dor, Taanach, and Megiddo on your map. Label this section of land MANASSEH and color it dark orange. This was the inheritance of the tribe of Manasseh.

Read **Joshua 17:14-18.**

Have you ever been involved in overseeing a large group of people? When major decisions are made, it is inevitable that someone will feel slighted. I love Joshua's comments. "If you are so numerous and if the hill country of Ephraim is too small for you, go up into the forest and clear land for yourselves there." Ha! I'm sure that went over like a lead balloon! The tribes of Ephraim and Manasseh wanted more land. Joshua held his position though, and let them know the allotment was final. This was their inheritance, and if they needed more livable land, they needed to clear it themselves.

Look again at **verse 16.** What was distinctive about the Canaanites in the area of Beth Shan and the Valley of Jezreel?

_____

Could this be the real reason that these tribes were unhappy with their allotment? What did God tell the Israelites in **Deuteronomy 20:1?**

_____
_____
_____
_____

These tribes were motivated by fear. What did Joshua say to the tribes in **Joshua 17:18?**

_____
_____
_____
_____

They could drive the Canaanites out because the same God who brought the ten plagues on the Egyptians, who brought the Israelites out of Egypt, and who parted the Red Sea is the same God who would empower them to drive out the Canaanites, just as He promised. The question was not whether the Israelites could drive them out. The question was: Would they? Look back at **verses 12-13.**

Sadly, they didn't. Even when the Israelites grew stronger in their faith, they only forced the Canaanites to be slaves. They didn't muster up the courage, or faith, to drive them out completely.

Read **Joshua 18:1-2**.

Do you remember the Tent of Meeting God had Moses construct so He could dwell among His people?

Look back at **Exodus 40:36-38**. What would indicate the Israelites were to move camp?_____

_____

Don't you find it interesting that God would choose to have the Israelites change camp and move into the heart of the Promised Land, right in the middle of allotting the land to the Israelites?

Read **Deuteronomy 12:13-14** below:

> *Be careful not to sacrifice your burnt offerings anywhere you please. Offer them only at the place the Lord will choose in one of your tribes, and there observe everything I command you.*

The tribe of God's choosing had received its inheritance, and He wasted no time in having the Tent of Meeting moved to its designated place.

Read **Joshua 18:3-10**.

Joshua needed more information before he could continue distributing the land. He might have been a little disturbed by the dispute that took place with Ephraim and Manasseh. He made it clear that from that point forward all lots would be cast in the presence of the Lord.

In tomorrow's lesson, we will witness the distribution of the land to the final seven tribes. Have your map pencils ready!

week 9 · day 4

ALLOTTED PORTIONS

These are the territories that Eleazar the priest, Joshua son of Nun and the heads of the tribal clans of Israel assigned by lot at Shiloh in the presence of the Lord at the entrance to the Tent of Meeting. And so they finished dividing the land.
Joshua 19:51

Today, we will plot the inheritance of the final seven tribes on our map. The tribes of Reuben, Gad, Judah, Ephraim and Manasseh have received their land; the Tent of Meeting was relocated to Shiloh; and the unallocated land had been surveyed to determine the inheritance of the remaining tribes.

Begin by reading **Joshua 18:11, 21-28.**

Locate the cities of Jericho, Bethel, Gibeon, and Mizpah on your map. Label this section of land BENJAMIN and color it yellow. This was the inheritance of the tribe of Benjamin.

Read **Joshua 19:1-9.**

Locate Beersheba, Hormah, and Ziklag on your map. Label this section of land SIMEON and color it brown. This was the inheritance of the tribe of Simeon.

Of the seven tribes, Simeon was the smallest. Yet, it appears that they were allotted more land than the tribe of Benjamin. The size of inheritance may have had more to do with the number of cities than actual territory.

How many towns were included in Benjamin's land? _____ (Joshua 18:24, 28)

How many towns were included in Simeon's land? _____ (Joshua 19:6-7)

It makes sense that Benjamin would receive more territory. However, the basis for allotment does not continue to be easy to understand.

Read **Joshua 19:10-16.**

Locate the cities of Daberath and Rimmon on your map. Label this section of land ZEBULUN and color it violet. This was the inheritance of the tribe of Zebulun.

Read **Joshua 19:17-23**.

Locate Mount Tabor and the city of Jezreel on your map. Label this section of land ISSACHAR and color it light brown. This was the inheritance of the tribe of Issachar.

Read **Joshua 19:24-31**.

Locate the city of Tyre on your map. This territory meets Zebulun's land and also has one boundary of the Great Sea. Label this section of land ASHER and color it black. This was the inheritance of the tribe of Asher.

Read **Joshua 19:32-39**.

Locate the cities of Hazor, Kedesh, and Ijon (Iron in the text) on your map. Notice that this land touches Zebulun's. Asher's land is the western boundary and the Jordan River is the eastern boundary. Label this section of land NAPHTALI and color it light orange. This was the inheritance of the tribe of Naphtali.

Read **Joshua 19:40-48**.

Locate the city of Joppa on your map. Label this section of land DAN and color it blue. This was the inheritance of the tribe of Dan.

Issachar was a fairly large tribe, yet they received what appears to be a very small piece of land. Even Simeon (the smallest tribe) received more. Perhaps the presence of a permanent spring made one piece of land more desirable than another. Water was a precious commodity since rainfall was minimal, so there may have been some emphasis on the amount of water a territory contained. Whatever the logic behind each tribe's allotted inheritance, the decisions were made in the presence of the Lord.

Sometimes God seems to provide more to some and less to others, with no logical explanation. Some of the tribes may have felt God's provision for them was too small. Others may have been frustrated with their lack of water or pasture land.

Have you have ever been envious because you felt God provided for others more abundantly than for you? If so, briefly describe how you felt.

_____

_____

_____

_____

Read **Isaiah 55:8** and **Proverbs 3:5-6**.

When life doesn't seem to make sense, we have to trust in the sovereignty of God. He often has purposes we can't understand. But if we acknowledge and trust Him in all our ways, he will make our journey far less bumpy and eventually enable us to be content with our circumstances.

Now read **Joshua 19:49-51**.

After all of the tribes had received their land, Joshua received an inheritance among them. What was the name of the town Joshua asked for (**v. 50**)?

_____

Timnath Serah was located in a rugged, infertile mountain area within Ephraim.[33] So why did Joshua choose that particular location? Perhaps the answer lies with the meaning of the town name. The Hebrew name for this town is Timnath Cherec. It means "portion of the sun."

Joshua would not have considered a location from a territory outside his own tribe. I can just picture the sparkle in his eye as Joshua came across "portion of the sun" in the land of Ephraim. Joshua had asked God to cause the sun to stand still over Gibeon, and his request was granted. I imagine he treasured that day above all others. Now Joshua would bask in his "portion of the sun" and in the memory of God's faithfulness for the remainder of his days.

Write **Psalm 37:4**.

_____

_____

_____

_____

What a precious memorial Joshua's "portion of the sun" must have been!

Through the lessons this week, what evidence did you find of God's faithfulness?

_____

_____

_____

_____

_____

week 9 · day 5

PERSONAL APPLICATION

The Reubenites, Gadites, and the half tribe of Manasseh were the first tribes to receive their land. As believers in Christ, we too receive a portion of our inheritance here on earth.

Read **Ephesians 1:13-14:**

> *You also were included in Christ when you heard the word of truth, the gospel of your salvation. Having believed, you were marked in him with a seal, the promised Holy Spirit, who is a **deposit guaranteeing our inheritance** until the redemption of those who are God's possession – to the praise of his glory.* (emphasis added)

In Greek, the words translated "deposit guaranteeing" are one word, *arrhabon*, which means "a pledge, part of the purchase-money, or property given in advance as security for the rest, earnest."

For Christians, the Holy Spirit is the portion of God we can experience here on earth. He is the deposit (portion of our inheritance given up front) that guarantees the remainder (eternal life in fellowship with our Father in heaven) will be granted at redemption.

Take a moment to thank God for this incredible deposit for you to hold on to.

The tribe of Ephraim never completely eliminated the Canaanites from their territory as God directed. Let's see what Scripture says about the consequences of disobedience. Read **Romans 6:11-22.**

The shame many of us carry is a direct result of allowing ourselves to become slaves to sin. We reap no benefit, only consequences and regret. So why do we resist the idea of becoming a slave to righteousness?

Read **Luke 6:46-49.**

Commit to being a "slave" to God, walking in obedience to the best of your ability. As you put the Word of God into practice, your life will be built on the solid foundation of the Rock. When the winds of temptation and adversity blow hard against you, you will not be shaken. Praise the Lord!

day three

God made His dwelling place among His people right after the territory had been allotted to Ephraim. The tabernacle was the earthly place where the Spirit of God dwelled.

Read **1 Corinthians 6:19-20.**

The Spirit of God now dwells in our bodies and we are to honor Him by living as slaves to righteousness. Our lives should be set apart and distinctive from the world around us.

Write a prayer committing to live as a slave to righteousness. Ask God to make you keenly aware of any sin or act that prevents close fellowship with Him.

_____

_____

_____

_____

_____

_____

_____

day four

For his inheritance, Joshua chose a town named "portion of the sun." He must have considered his inheritance to be worth more than any lush, fertile ground available in the Promised Land. Joshua's inheritance represented proof God listened to him and acted on his behalf.

Can you recall a time when God granted your request in a tangible way? If so, describe the circumstances.

_____

_____

_____

_____

Read **Philippians 4:6.** Is there a request you want to make of God, but feel it is too bold, or too much to ask?

_____

If God could grant Joshua additional hours in the day, He is certainly able to answer your requests. Go ahead, ask Him. He delights in your prayers! (**Proverbs 15:8**)

Read **Psalm 86:1-7** as a prayer. He will answer you in His way and in His time!

CLAIMING THE PROMISE

My God will meet all your needs according to

his glorious riches in Christ Jesus.

PHILIPPIANS 4:19

week 10 • day 1

A PLACE OF REFUGE

week 10 • day 2

FAITHFUL PROVISION

week 10 • day 3

RETURNING HOME

week 10 • day 4

MISSION ACCOMPLISHED

week 10 • day 5

PERSONAL APPLICATION

A PLACE OF REFUGE

Tell the Israelites to designate the cities of refuge, as I instructed you through Moses.
Joshua 20:2

Last week we plotted each tribe's inheritance on our map and saw that God was faithful to provide for the Israelites, just as He promised. With the task of allotting the land behind him, Joshua was called on to set up the cities of refuge.

Read **Numbers 35:6-8.**

According to **verse 6**, what was the purpose of a city of refuge?

_____

Moses had designated three cities of refuge on the east side of the Jordan. Read **Deuteronomy 4:41-43** and write the names of the three cities:

_____ for the Reubenites; _____ for the Gadites; and _____ for the Manassites.

Let's see which cities Joshua chose as the cities of refuge in Canaan. Read **Joshua 20:1-9.** Write the names of the cities:

_____ _____ _____

Draw a small circle around each of the six cities of refuge on your map, then read **Deuteronomy 19:1-7.**

The avenger of blood was the nearest male relative of a victim. He was responsible for taking revenge by putting a killer to death. The accused could only find refuge within the walls of these designated cities.

Read **Deuteronomy 19:8-13.**

Had the Israelites carefully followed God's laws, He would have enlarged their territory. According to **verse 9**, what were the laws they were required to follow?

_____ and _____

The Israelites' territory was never enlarged. They didn't continue to love God and walk in His ways in the land of their inheritance.

If God were to assess your life up to this time based on these standards, do you think He would enlarge your territory? If so, ask Him to prepare you to handle the growth. If not, is the problem your love for the Lord, your walk, or both?

_____

Read **1 Chronicles 4:9-10.**

The name Jabez sounds like the Hebrew word for pain. Jabez's mother gave him a name that would forever associate him with pain. He cried out to God to change his destiny. He asked God to enlarge his territory, to be with him, and to keep him from causing pain. What does verse 10 say God did?

_____

Ask God to enlarge your territory by enabling you to reach out and be a light to more of God's people. Ask Him to transform your life into a blessing, regardless of how others may have viewed you in the past. If you have a heart to serve God, I promise you, He will not waste it!

A killer would flee to a city of refuge and seek asylum there. If the death had been an accident, he could remain in the city. But if he had killed intentionally, he was turned over to the avenger to be killed as restitution.

Interestingly, a synonym for the word *avenging* is *unforgiving*. The law given to Moses was unforgiving in that it called for judgment and death without mercy. As believers, we find refuge from the avenging law that condemns us for our sin.

Read **Hebrews 6:13-20.**

God's promise to Abraham was absolute, for He swore by Himself and it is impossible for God to lie. Likewise, God's promise of salvation is absolute for those who have fled to take refuge in Christ. We are assured protection from the condemnation of the avenging law. We can live in the safety of Christ forever.

Write **Romans 8:1.** _____

_____

_____

The Hebrew word for avenger, *ga'al*, is often translated "redeemer." An avenger of blood took revenge against his brother's killer as payment for the sin. In contrast, our Redeemer brought forgiveness and became the payment for our sins.

Read **Job 19:25-27** out loud.

Your Redeemer and High Priest lives forever in heaven. One day you will see His glorious face with your very own eyes.

week 10 · day 2

FAITHFUL PROVISION

My God will meet all your needs according to his glorious riches in Christ Jesus.
Philippians 4:19

God faithfully provided towns and pasturelands for the Levites, just as He promised. The Levites were responsible for serving at and caring for the Tent of Meeting. God Himself was their inheritance. He provided for their needs by giving them all the tithes of Israel, and towns to live in within the other tribes' territories.

Read **Numbers 35:1-3.**

Joshua and the other leaders honored God's command. Read all of **Joshua 21.** (You may want to underline the names of the towns listed in order to keep your bearings.)

The Levites received forty-eight towns disbursed throughout the Israelites' territory. It's been estimated that no one in Israel lived more than ten miles from a Levite town.[34] Thus, the Levites were able to effectively teach God's laws to the people and counsel them as needed. At this time, people didn't have direct access to God's Word as we do today. The priests were responsible for teaching and interpreting the law for the people.

We are incredibly blessed to own a copy of the Bible. We shouldn't take that privilege for granted. Rather than depending on pastors and teachers to read us God's Word, we need to read our Bibles and study the Word for ourselves.

How many Bibles do you own? _____

Stop for a moment to thank God for granting you access to His precious Word through the technology of our times. We can purchase a copy of the Bible in any bookstore. We can also access it on the Internet or through Bible software. We even have our choice of numerous translations and formats.

God commanded the Israelites to be faithful to the law while living in Canaan.

Read **Deuteronomy 4:5-8.**

The Israelites were to serve as witnesses to other nations. If the Israelites faithfully followed God's law, others would recognize the God of Israel was different from the false gods they worshiped. He was with His people!

According to **verse 7**, when is God near to us?

_____

Do you sense God's presence when you pray? If so, praise Him for blessing you with His holy presence. If not, take a moment to try again. Close your eyes to block out distractions. Take a minute to sit quietly and relax. Talk to God about any struggles or difficulties you're having. Ask Him to reveal Himself to you.

I love those who love me, and those who seek me find me.
Proverbs 8:17

We are called to be witnesses to others. Write down the name of one Christian brother or sister whose life is a witness to you on a regular basis. How has this person impacted you?

_____
_____
_____
_____
_____
_____

God provided the Levites to help His people remain faithful to Him and receive His blessings. Do you believe God will provide everything you need today? Read **Philippians 4:19** and rewrite it, personalizing it.

_____
_____
_____
_____

God says He will provide for you. Spend some prayer time and thank Him for His faithfulness to provide for His people, both physically and spiritually. Ask Him to provide for you just as He did for the Israelites.

> *Because of the Lord's great love we are not consumed,*
> *for his compassions never fail.*
> *They are new every morning;*
> *great is your faithfulness.*
> *I say to myself, "The Lord is my portion;*
> *therefore I will wait for him."*
> *The Lord is good to those whose hope is in him,*
> *to the one who seeks him.*

Lamentations 3:22-25

RETURNING HOME

Now that the Lord your God has given your brothers rest as he promised,
return to your homes in the land that Moses the servant of the Lord gave you
on the other side of the Jordan.
Joshua 22:4

All the land had been assigned. God had fulfilled His promises to the Israelites.
It was now seven long years since they had crossed the Jordan to claim their
inheritance.[35]

Read **Joshua 22:1-8.**

The Reubenites, Gadites and the half tribe of Manasseh had been away from
their families for seven years. They hadn't deserted their brothers; they had
completed the mission the Lord gave them. Joshua blessed them, and out of his
love and concern for their long-term well-being, he passionately urged them to
keep God's commandments.

They must have experienced many emotions as they prepared to return to the
east side of the Jordan. I'm sure they were eager to see their families. Many of
their children would have grown to adulthood in the time they were away. Yet
they had certainly developed many bonds with the men in other tribes. They had
overcome great obstacles and experienced God's miraculous provision together.
There must have been a deep brotherhood among all the Israelites. Leaving had
to have been difficult.

Have you ever experienced this type of separation from family or friends? If so,
describe the circumstances and some of the emotions you felt at the time.

_____

_____

_____

_____

_____

_____

Trouble was brewing. Read **Joshua 22:9-14.**

The Israelites were furious at the idea that their brothers would set up an altar other than the one located at Shiloh. Let's see why they were so upset.

Read **Deuteronomy 12:1-14.**

Where were the Israelites to bring their offerings (**v. 14**)?

_____

_____

_____

_____

The tribes in Canaan loved these men; they were fellow Israelites. They had fought by their sides for years. But they were willing to go to war to defend the principles and laws of their God.

The Israelites west of the Jordan were jumping to conclusions. Thankfully, Joshua was wise in his handling of the situation. Rather than attacking based on rumor, he sent Phinehas (Aaron's grandson) along with tribal leaders to talk with the eastern tribes.

Now Phinehas was an interesting choice. How is he described in **Numbers 25:5-11**?

_____

Phinehas would not have been afraid to act. He was probably still just as zealous for honor among God's people as he had ever been. These men knew of Phinehas' actions in Moab. His presence would have sent a strong message.

Read **Joshua 22:15-20.** You can almost feel the intensity as you read.

What offer did the western Israelite leaders make to the Reubenites, Gadites, and the half tribe of Manasseh (**v. 19**)?

_____

Their love was evident by the sacrifice they were willing to make in order to keep unity between tribes.

Read **Joshua 22:21-34.**

The eastern tribes were trying to ensure unity and security for their descendants. They were insecure in their position across the Jordan so they wanted to set up a memorial as a replica of the true altar to serve as a reminder that all twelve tribes worshiped the same God. These tribes were bound by their love for the Lord, and the altar served as a reminder that the Lord was God of all Israel.

week 10 • day 4

MISSION ACCOMPLISHED

He brought out his people with rejoicing, his chosen ones with shouts of joy;
he gave them the lands of the nations, and they fell heir to what others had
toiled for – that they might keep his precepts and observe his laws. Praise the Lord.
Psalm 105:43-45

Today we will witness Joshua's formal farewell to the Israelite leaders and
say good-bye to the faithful man of God we've journeyed with to the land of
Promise. In his final address, Joshua made a strong appeal to the Israelites,
urging them to remain faithful to the one true God. He assembled the Israelites
at the familiar site of Shechem and renewed the covenant between God and His
people.

Read all of **Joshua 23** out loud. Try to picture the scene as you read.

Joshua pleaded with the Israelites in an attempt to alter the path God revealed
they would take in Canaan. His passion and love for these people is admirable.
He reminded them of the consequences of breaking covenant with God by
turning to other gods. He desperately wanted the Israelites to be faithful. Why?
Because God is faithful and worthy of loyalty and devotion from His people.

If a portion of your church congregation turned away from the Lord and began
worshiping a god of another religion, what are some of things you would say in
an effort to convince them to remain faithful to the one true God?

_____

_____

_____

_____

_____

_____

_____

_____

_____

The key to impacting others is instructing them with love. The people knew Joshua loved them. They also knew he had a real and intimate relationship with God. These relationships gave him credibility.

Have you ever strayed from God? If so, was there someone who was instrumental in leading you back? What did this person do to help you?

_____

_____

_____

_____

Take a few minutes and write that person a note to thank them.

Joshua assembled all of Israel at Shechem. He reminded everyone of all they had been through and of God's faithfulness throughout their journey. They probably read the law at this gathering. If so, they would have been in their usual formation on Mt. Ebal and Mt. Gerizim.

Read **Joshua 24:1-13**.

God had sent the Canaanites running as if they were being chased by hornets. He gave the Israelites cities that were already built and vineyards already planted. God had driven the people of Canaan out before them in battle, and He met every need they had.

Read **Joshua 24:14-15** out loud.

Choose for yourselves this day whom you will serve!

Oswald Chambers put it this way:

> *The proposition is between you and God; do not confer with flesh and blood about it. With every new proposition other people get more and more "out of it" – that is where the strain comes. God allows the opinion of His saints to matter to you, and yet you are brought more and more out of the certainty that others understand the step you are taking. You have no business to find out where God is leading, the only thing God will explain to you is Himself. Profess to Him – "I will be loyal."* [36]

Are you willing to commit to this type of devotion and loyalty to God?

_____

Read **Joshua 24:16-27**.

Once again Joshua stood on the holy spot where God first promised the land to the Israelites. He took a large stone and placed it under the historical oak. The stone was a witness to them, testifying to the fact that they had heard the words of the Lord. If they chose to deny Him, it would be a choice to rebel against His commands.

Read **Joshua 24:28-33**.

Having completed his final act as leader, Joshua sent the people home. He was buried in his "Portion of the Sun" at the age of 110. The Israelites remained faithful to God as long as the elders who had served under Joshua lived.

Read **Genesis 50:24-26**.

The Israelites kept their vow to Joseph and carried his bones throughout their long journey. They were finally laid to rest, just as Joseph had requested.

God is so faithful! What evidence did you find of His faithfulness this week?

_____
_____
_____
_____
_____
_____
_____

In conclusion, read **Psalm 105**. Read slowly and ponder the events we've studied. Praise Him for His faithfulness as you read.

PERSONAL APPLICATION

day one

The Israelites found protection in the designated cities of refuge. We find shelter by seeking refuge in Christ.

Read **Psalm 57:1**.

The Hebrew word translated "refuge" in this verse is *chacah*. It means "to flee for protection; figuratively, to confide in."

Now read all of **Psalm 4**.

The Hebrew word translated "trust" in verse 5 is *batach*. It means "to hide for refuge; figuratively, to trust, be confident or sure."

These words are translated either as "to trust" or "to take refuge in" throughout the Old Testament. There is a clear link between the level of trust we have for the Lord and our ability to seek Him for shelter in times of trouble.

If we seek refuge in something other than the Lord, the underlying problem is a lack of trust in God. Below are a few "somethings" we can flee to for protection other than the Lord. Circle the "something" (or write in your own) that you most often flee to rather than seeking refuge in the Lord.

WORK   ALCOHOL   FOOD   FRIENDS   SLEEP   PARENTS   OTHER: _____

The next time you face stress, tragedy, or persecution, sit down with your Bible and read the Psalms out loud. Ask God to comfort you with His Word. Or turn on praise music and worship with all of your heart before the Lord. If you enjoy being outside, take a long walk and pray. Whatever the method, God is able to protect and comfort you. Anything else is simply a substitute. It may bring temporary comfort, but it will offer no lasting protection.

Read **Hebrews 7:24-25**.

You can abide in the shelter of Christ forever because our High Priest lives forever!

day two

Every Israelite had the opportunity to seek the wisdom of the Levites and priests who lived among them.

Today, one of the biggest lies Satan dupes Christians into believing is that they do not need to regularly attend church to have a deep and growing relationship with the Lord.

Read **John 21:15-17** and **I Thessalonians 5:10-11**.

There are numerous benefits to being involved in a local church body.

- We display the love we have for Christ by serving His people (feeding His sheep).

- Every believer has God-given gifts and talents intended to be used to further His kingdom. We waste those gifts if we don't use them for their intended purpose.

- We benefit from the wisdom and insight of other believers.

- Our faith is strengthened by witnessing God's work through others.

You need to be active and serving in a church. Don't allow Satan to convince you otherwise.

Are you regularly attending a church at this time? If so, what are some ways that you have been positively impacted by your involvement?

_____

_____

_____

_____

_____

_____

day three

The eastern Israelites built a memorial to serve as a witness that the Israelites from both sides of the Jordan were united because they worshiped the same God.

God desires that His people be unified by their devotion to Him. Sadly, Sunday morning is the most divided day of the week. Even beyond denominational differences, we see racial and ethnic segregation. "Whites" go to "white" churches, "blacks" go to "black" churches. There are Chinese churches, Indian churches, Hispanic churches, and more. Congregations that reach beyond these barriers are a rare treasure.

I'd like to share a poem I wrote as I grieved over the brutal death of a man named James Byrd several years ago in Jasper, Texas. He was dragged behind a vehicle by three white men simply because of the color of his skin. My heart ached at the hatred and pride that still exists between many people of different races and cultures. This poem came from my prayers at that time.

Blinded

Lord, I'm brought to my knees by the hatred I see,
By the walls that divide, and the fears that they breed.
You make no mistakes, each child's a masterpiece.
Somehow we've been blinded by the colors we see.

Lord, touch our hearts to look up to Thee,
For the strength to breakdown walls of hostility,
To see each as a blessing to all humanity.
Somehow we've been blinded by the colors we see.

Some need to know how or why this could be,
Each made in Your image, yet so differently.
Lord, give us Your eyes, to see as You see.
Somehow we've been blinded by the colors we see.

Forgive us the sin that hides the mystery,
Take the scales from our eyes and allow us to see,
Your death on the cross brought us all unity.
Lord, unveil the blessing in the colors we see.

Spend a few moments in prayer and ask God to allow you to see as He sees.

Read **Psalm 18:29**.

This is such a complicated issue that we may never fully understand it. The walls that divide God's people have been built, brick by brick, over countless generations. The pain runs deep, and the pride thick. It makes my heart ache to realize how far we still have to go.

Oh, how we should desire to be united by the commonality of our love for God, by our need for Christ, and by the frailty of our human condition. To scale the walls that divide God's people, we need to earnestly pray for God to change the hearts of every man, woman, and child in our nation. God is truly the only source of complete reconciliation. But we must do our best to reach out to people of other races, embracing our differences.

If you have prejudices against people of another race or culture, confess it as the sin that it is and ask God to help you scale the walls that divide us.

Have you ever been treated in an unkind manner due to a stereotype or assumption that someone made because of your appearance or association? If so, describe your feelings.

_____

_____

_____

_____

_____

_____

Have you ever made an assumption about someone, only to find you were wrong once you got to know the person? Briefly describe the circumstances.

_____

Ask God to use these experiences to help you better understand people of a different race or background from yours.

day four

Joshua said good-bye to the people he had faithfully led to the Promised Land. We saw him struggle with fear in the early stages of his walk with God. But we also watched him grow into a mighty warrior for the Lord.

What did God teach you through our study of Joshua?

_____
_____
_____
_____
_____
_____
_____
_____
_____
_____
_____

What did you learn about God by seeing Him through the eyes of Joshua?

_____
_____
_____
_____
_____
_____
_____
_____
_____
_____
_____

LIVING THE PROMISE

If you belong to Christ, then you are Abraham's seed,
and heirs according to the promise.

GALATIANS 3:29

week 11 • day 1

ABRAHAM'S SEED

week 11 • day 2

THE SEAL

week 11 • day 3

FRUITFULNESS

week 11 • day 4

A FRUITFUL TASK

week 11 • day 5

THE PROMISED LAND

week 11 · day 1

ABRAHAM'S SEED

If you belong to Christ, then you are Abraham's seed,
and heirs according to the promise.
Galatians 3:29

Today we will revisit the original covenant God made with Abraham and trace the lineage of Christ to verify His identity as the "Seed" God promised would bless all nations.

Begin by reading **Genesis 17:1-8.**

The KING JAMES VERSION translates **verse 7** as follows:

*I will establish my covenant between me and thee and **thy seed** after thee*
in their generations for an everlasting covenant, to be a God unto thee,
and to thy seed after thee. (emphasis added)

Now read **Genesis 22:17-18.**

The word *offspring* in **verse 18** is the Hebrew word *zera*, which means "seed; figuratively, fruit." It is translated "seed" in the KING JAMES VERSION.

According to verse 18, who will be blessed by Abraham's seed?

_____

Read **Galatians 3:15-25** for Paul's explanation of the use of the word *seed*.

The law was established to lead us to Christ so that all nations would be released from the bondage of the law. Christ is the Seed God referred to in His covenant promise to Abraham. Let's trace Christ's genealogy and verify that, indeed, He is the Seed of Abraham.

Take a moment to glance at **Matthew 1:1-16.**

This is the genealogy of Christ through his legal father, Joseph. Jesus wasn't Joseph's blood descendant because he was conceived by the Holy Spirit and born to the virgin Mary. But this genealogy proves Jesus was a legal heir of Abraham.

Which son of David is listed in **Matthew 1:6**?

_____

_____

Compare this genealogy to the one in **Luke 3:23-38**.

Which son of David is listed in **Luke 3:31**? (Note: This list is in ascending order, whereas Matthew's account was descending order.)

_____

_____

In Matthew's account, Solomon is listed as an ancestor of Joseph. In Luke's account, it is Nathan. That is because Matthew gave Joseph's line; Luke listed Mary's line. Mary's genealogy, in accordance with Jewish custom, was in her husband's name.[37] Jesus was a descendant of Abraham legally through Joseph, and by bloodline through Mary. He is the Seed through whom all nations are blessed.

So what's the blessing? Let's look. What did God promise Abraham in **Genesis 17:7**?

_____

_____

God promised to be the God of all Abraham's descendants.

Now read **Galatians 3:26-29**.

God provided a means for you to be adopted into the family of His covenant people through your faith in His Son. Let's take a look at additional proof of Jesus' identity as the Seed of Abraham.

Read **Luke 2:4-11**.

Who did the angel say his good news was for (**v. 10**)?

_____

_____

Christ came to bring the good news of salvation to all people.

Re-read **Galatians 3:29** and write it.

_____

_____

_____

_____

You are an heir with Christ to God's precious promises.

Now read **Galatians 4:1-7**.

Until the appointed time, God's children were subject to the law. But because of Christ, we have been adopted into God's family and we have all the rights of a son. We are able to call Him Abba, which is an affectionate term Hebrew children called their fathers. Because of Christ, we get to call God "Daddy."

As a way of closing, take a moment to pray, addressing God as Abba or Daddy.

week 11 · day 2

THE SEAL

Having believed, you were marked in him with a seal,
the promised Holy Spirit.
Ephesians 1:13

Let's look back again today at the covenant God made with Abraham. Read
Genesis 17:7-11.

What was the sign of the covenant between God and Abraham?

_____

Read **Deuteronomy 10:12-20.**

In **verse 16,** what did Moses tell the Israelites to do?

_____

Moses gave examples of God's softhearted nature. He defends "the fatherless
and the widow," meets the needs of strangers, shows no partiality, and cannot
be bribed. Moses told the Israelites to cut back the hard covering of their hearts
and emulate the behavior of their Lord.

How sensitive are you to the needs of others? _____

What are some ways you can provide for the needy in your area?

_____

_____

_____

_____

_____

Circumcision was intended to be a physical sign of what had taken place in the
hearts of God's people.

Read **Romans 3:27-4:17.**

Abraham received circumcision as a seal of righteousness – an outward sign of the faith he had in God's promise. We too receive a "seal" that is a sign of the faith we have already professed. Read **Ephesians 1:11-14**.

The Holy Spirit is the Christian's sign that we are heirs with Christ. Let's spend the rest of this lesson looking at the role of the Holy Spirit on our spiritual journey.

Read John **14:15-17**. How long will the Holy Spirit be with you?

_____

According to **verse 17** where does the Spirit reside?

_____

The Holy Spirit resides in the hearts of believers, and He will be with us forever.

Read **John 7:37-39**.

The Holy Spirit is like living water that flows from believers when they are doing the will of God. If you've ever experienced the Spirit in this manner, you know what Jesus was talking about. The Spirit enables you to pour out the love of God on others. You become "like a tree, planted by streams of water" (**Psalm 1:3**) and are empowered to accomplish far more than you could ever accomplish on your own.

Have you ever had an experience where the Holy Spirit enabled you to accomplish something beyond your own capabilities? If so, explain.

_____

_____

_____

_____

_____

Read **John 14:23-26**. What does the Holy Spirit do for us (**v. 26**)?

_____

_____

The Holy Spirit works together with the Word of God to teach us. He reminds us of Christ's words and applies them to situations we face. To fully experience the power of the Holy Spirit, we must read the Word of God. By reading and studying the Word, we feed God's Spirit, which dwells within us, and increase His power in our lives.

During Spiritual Boot Camp we learned about the importance of memorizing Scripture. The Word is the weapon we use to battle the lies of our enemy. Living without the Word is like entering a battlefield unarmed.

The Holy Spirit is referred to in **John 14:26** as the "Counselor." In Old Testament times counselors were members of the king's court and acted as advisors. In New Testament times counselors were members of advisory or legislative committees.[38] For the Christian, the Holy Spirit acts as an advisor, giving us insight into the deep meanings of Scripture. That insight causes God's Word to have deeper meaning and significance.

Through this study, has the Holy Spirit given you a more indepth understanding of some of the truths contained in God's Word? If so, give an example.

_____

_____

_____

_____

_____

_____

_____

_____

We've talked about feeding the Spirit and increasing His power. Now, let's briefly look at ways Scripture tells us we push Him down and shrink His presence.

Read **Ephesians 4:30–5:4**. According to these verses what are some ways we can grieve the Holy Spirit?

_____

_____

_____

_____

Spend a few minutes in prayer and reflection. Ask God to reveal ways you have been grieving the Holy Spirit. Write any changes you need to make.

_____

_____

_____

_____

_____

Read **Luke 11:13**. Ask Him to bless you with His presence!

week 11 • day 3

FRUITFULNESS

You did not choose me, but I chose you and appointed you to go
and bear fruit – fruit that will last.
John 15:16

Let's look once again at the covenant between God and Abraham. Today we will focus on God's promise to make Abraham's descendants fruitful.

Read **Genesis 17:1-6** once again.

The Hebrew word translated as "fruitful" in this passage is *parah*. It means "to bear fruit; bring forth fruit; to be, cause to be, make fruitful, grow, increase."

As Abraham's descendants, we share in this promise to be fruitful. Let's take a closer look at what that means.

Read **John 15:1-4**.

Jesus is the vine, so in order to bear fruit we must remain securely attached to Him. God prunes us (cuts back the undesirable shoots that grow out of control) in order to make us more fruitful.

How do you think you remain attached to the vine?

_____
_____
_____
_____
_____

To remain attached to Christ, we must be in an intimate relationship with Him. We build a strong relationship with Jesus the same way we develop all relationships – by spending time with Him. Establishing daily prayer time is an important element of our relationship. When we remain securely attached to the vine, the life-giving water (the Holy Spirit) is able to sufficiently flow from Christ to us, so we can flourish and grow.

Are you willing to allow God to prune away the elements of your life that are out of control?

_____

The process of pruning is sometimes a bit painful. But by allowing God to prune us, we are more fruitful and increase the effectiveness of the Holy Spirit.

Now read **John 15:5-8**.

What does **verse 8** say your fruitfulness reveals?

_____

We reveal to the world that we are disciples by the fruit we bear. The greatest fruit we can produce on this earth is another disciple. If all we do is introduce others to Christ, we are doing a good work. We are spreading the good news. But Jesus told us to do more than that. He said, "Go and make disciples of all nations" (**Matthew 28:19**).

If we take a new believer under our wing, teach them, encourage them, and help them become wholly devoted to God, we have helped them become attached to the vine so that they too can bear fruit.

Read **John 15:9-17**.

According to **verse 16**, what has Christ appointed you to do?

_____

Bear fruit that lasts. As a disciple, get involved in the lives of other believers.

Spend a few minutes in prayer. Ask God to reveal ways you can build up other believers and help them become wholly devoted disciples. Write any ideas that come to you during this prayer time.

_____

_____

_____

_____

_____

Are you committed to developing the heart of a wholly devoted disciple? If not, spend a few minutes in prayer and ask God to reveal what is holding you back. Write anything that He reveals.

_____

_____

_____

_____

_____

_____

_____

_____

_____

God desires for us to be fruitful disciples, fully yielded to Him as we inspire others to do the same.

FRUITFUL TASK

I will make you very fruitful.
Genesis 17:6

As Abraham's spiritual descendants, we are appointed by Christ to bear fruit. The greatest work we perform as Christ's disciples is raising up other disciples. In doing this, we are being spiritually fruitful in the same sense that Abraham was fruitful when God physically multiplied his descendants.

Read **Revelation 7:9.**

Palm trees represent fruitfulness and the blessings of God. Why do you think the multitude waved them before the throne and in front of the Lamb?

_____

_____

_____

_____

_____

One day we will wave our palm branches as we celebrate the ultimate fulfillment of God's covenant promise through Christ. Our palm branches will represent our fruitful acts on this earth.

The Lord has specific tasks for you to perform to build His kingdom. I believe every circumstance and trial you have experienced was allowed by God to prepare you and strengthen you for those tasks. Discovering your divine assignments may take time, but ask God. He will reveal what He would have you to do.

I'd like to share the experience I had as I began writing this study. When I sensed God moving me to write, I experienced some of the same emotions Moses experienced when God first told him to lead the Israelites out of Egypt.

At that time I had never taught a single lesson of my own material. I had facilitated a woman's Sunday school class with prepared material, but I hadn't taught straight from the Word of God. I'd never written anything of substance in my life. Other than my love for the Word of God and my passion to do whatever God wanted me to do, I had absolutely no qualifications.

I considered it absurd to think God wanted me to write a Bible study. After spending a number of days in prayer, I continued to sense this was something God wanted me to do.

I had tremendous doubts about my ability to teach. I felt inadequate (and even a little foolish). At that time, God prompted a precious woman in my Sunday school class to send me a note. Here is a portion of what she said.

> You are a special person in my life because you are a teacher. My definition of a teacher is someone who is willing to admit and share her shortcomings and sin in order that others may learn and grow from her experiences…Thank you so much for being willing to share with us and be our teacher.

I was so thankful for that sweet woman's encouragement, I decided to sit down in obedience before the computer and see what happened. The information God revealed to me as I studied and wrote inspired me. But after writing two weeks of lessons, I began to once again have tremendous doubts.

I went to a conference where a speaker talked of her own discouragement as a writer. She too had doubted God's call to write Bible studies. She talked of feeling foolish and embarrassed. This woman is the author of many published studies and it is obvious to all who have done them that she was indeed anointed by God to write them. As she talked about how she had overcome her feelings of inadequacy, she read **2 Corinthians 3:5**.

Write this verse below:

_____

_____

_____

_____

_____

I wept when I left that conference. I began writing and again prayerfully sought direction for the study. One morning as I was praying, I got the idea for the Spiritual Boot Camp portion of the study. I began to sense God wanted me to teach on spiritual warfare in the format of basic training. I knew nothing about military life, so I got a reference book on the subject. I asked God to lead me to the right book, and I located one the very next day.

God clearly and patiently confirmed what He wanted me to do through other believers, circumstances, and His Word. I depended on Him every day for the information, like manna from heaven.

I have seen the faithfulness of God through this experience unlike anything I have ever done. May my experience encourage you when God asks you to do something beyond your capabilities.

If God gives you a task, He will provide everything you need to complete it. I assure you, I did not write this Bible study on my own. The Holy Spirit worked through me to accomplish something that God wanted done to build up disciples for Christ. This study was as monumental to me as the parting of the Red Sea was for Moses.

Don't limit the God of all creation. If He allowed the Israelites to cross the Jordan on dry ground and made the sun stand still for Joshua, rest assured He will provide you with all you need to accomplish whatever task He gives you.

Be willing to put on the full armor of God, and when evil comes against you, stand firm. Remain tightly attached to Christ. Allow the living water of the Holy Spirit to flow through you to all God's children. You will come to know your God in a way you never dreamed possible!

Have I not commanded you? Be strong and courageous.
Do not be terrified; do not be discouraged,
for the Lord your God will be with you wherever you go.
Joshua 1:9

week 11 • day 5

THE PROMISED LAND

*Blessed are those who wash their robes, that they may have
the right to the tree of life and may go through the gates into the city.*
Revelation 22:14

It is difficult for me to believe this is our final lesson. I hope you have learned to trust in the faithfulness of God more deeply as a result of our study together. We have seen Joshua's mistakes and we have seen his victories. In both, we have seen a man wholly devoted to God.

Joshua's journey represents ours as we walk with God through this life on our way to our eternal Promised Land. Like Joshua, we can experience victory over our enemy when we faithfully seek the Lord and act according to His will. Like Joshua, our destiny is secure. Just as the Israelites were sure to inherit the Promised Land in Canaan, so our future residence in heaven is secure as spiritual descendants of Abraham through Christ.

Let's look one final time at the covenant between God and Abraham. Read **Genesis 17:8** below.

*The whole land of Canaan, where you are now an alien,
I will give as an everlasting possession
to you and your descendants after you; and I will be their God.*

God's ultimate fulfillment of this everlasting promise is our eternal residence in what Scripture calls "the New Jerusalem."

Read **Revelation 21:1-3.**

What does the voice from the throne say (**verse 3**)?

_____

_____

_____

_____

_____

We serve a faithful and mighty God! This covenant was an everlasting covenant in a way that was far beyond Abraham's comprehension. The New Jerusalem is the everlasting possession the descendants of Abraham will inherit, and we will be His people and He will be our God – *forever*.

Let's take a peek at that holy city. Read **Revelation 21:4-27**.

God is going to make *everything* new! He will be with us and will be our God; there will be no more darkness or pain; we will drink freely of the water of life (the Holy Spirit).

Read **Revelation 22:1-6**.

No longer will there be any curse from the fall that occurred in Eden. We will see the face of God, and His name will be on our foreheads. Our light will come from the Lord Himself. God and the Lamb will reign forever. Amen!

Read **John 14:2-3**.

Jesus is preparing the New Jerusalem. When He returns, He will take us to be with Him in our everlasting residence. As Jesus' bride, the church is making herself ready for the day when He returns. At that time there will be a glorious wedding supper.

Read **Revelation 19:6-9**.

You will wear "fine linen, bright and clean." You will be clothed in the beauty of the righteous acts you have done here on earth. Now, let's take a look at your bridegroom who, like a prince in a fairytale, rides in on a white horse.

Read **Revelation 19:11-14**.

At a Jewish wedding ceremony, it was customary for the bride and groom to share a cup of wine.[39] When did Jesus tell the disciples He would drink of the "fruit of the vine" again (**Luke 22:18**)?

_____

What a tender moment it will be when you share that cup of wine with your Savior!

Read **Revelation 22:12-17**.

With our robes washed in the blood of Christ, we will enter the gates of heaven and dwell in the New Jerusalem together with our Lord, drinking freely of the water of life. We will dance on those streets of gold (**Revelation 21:21**) and wave our palm branches before the Lamb.

As His bride, make yourself ready. He is coming soon!

What evidence did you find of God's faithfulness on this journey?

_____

_____

_____

_____

_____

What information in the study impacted you most?

_____

_____

_____

_____

_____

I have enjoyed taking this journey with you. I pray you have been as blessed by this study as I have.

Regardless of what trials you face as you walk with God on your way to our eternal home, hold tightly to the promises of our faithful God. Be strong and courageous, knowing the Lord your God will be with you wherever you go. Cling to the promise of what is yet to come.

I know that my Redeemer lives,
and that in the end he will stand upon the earth.

And after my skin has been destroyed,
yet in my flesh I will see God;

I myself will see him with my own eyes —
I and not another.

How my heart yearns within me!

Job 19:25-27

ENDNOTES

1 Merrill F Unger, *Concise Bible Dictionary*, (Tyndale House Publishers, Inc., 1974), 15.

2 *The New International Webster's Concise Dictionary of the English Language*, (Trident Press International, 1997), 616

3 Ginny Owens, "If You Want Me To" (*A Night In Rocketown*, 1999).

4 *Webster's New Compact Dictionary for School and Office*, (Thomas Nelson Publishers, Nashville, 1978), 98.

5 ibid., 226.

6 *NIV Student Bible*, (Zondervan Corporation, 1986) "Is War Ever Holy," 210-211.

7 Walvoord & Zuck, *The Bible Knowledge Commentary, Old Testament,* (Cook Communications Ministries, 2000), 1307.

8 Lee Strobel, *The Case for Christ*, (Zondervan Publishing House, 1998), 195.

9 Ibid, 197-198.

10 Merrill F. Unger, *Concise Bible Dictionary*, (Tyndale House Publishers, Inc. 1974), 108.

11 Walvoord and Zuck, *The Bible Knowledge Commentary, Old Testament,* (Cook Communications Ministries, 2000), 347.

12 Kay Arthur, *Our Covenant God* (Waterbrook Press, 1999), 74.

13 Walvoord & Zuck, *The Bible Knowledge Commentary,* (Cook Communications Ministries, Inc., 2000), 351.

14 *Webster's New Compact Dictionary for School and Office*, (Thomas Nelson Publishers, 1978), 293.

15 Walvoord & Zuck, *The Bible Knowledge Commentary, Old Testament,* (Cook Communications Ministries, 2000), 351

16 Ibid, 353.

17 *Webster's New Compact Dictionary for School and Office*, (Thomas Nelson Publishers, 1978), 65.

18 Peter Thompson, M.Ed., *The Real Insider's Guide to Military Basic Training,* (Universal Publishers/uPUBLISH.com, 1998), 55.

19 Ibid, 55.

20 Merrill F. Unger, *Concise Bible Dictionary*, (Tyndale House Publishers, Inc., 1974), 133.

21 The Student Bible, *"The Last Place to Start a Church"* (Zondervan Publishing, 1986), 1000.

22 Tony Evans, *The Battle is the Lord's,* (Moody Press, 1998), 265.

23 Merrill F. Unger, *Concise Bible Dictionary*, (Tyndale House Publishers, Inc., 1974), 164.

24 Tony Evans, *The Battle Is The Lords,* (Moody Press, 1998). 270.

25 Peter Thompson, M.Ed., *The Real Insider's Guide to Military Basic Training,* (Universal Publishers/uPUBLISH.com, 1998), 58.

26 Ibid, 58.

27 Merrill F. Unger, *Concise Bible Dictionary*, (Tyndale House Publishers, Inc., 1974), 90.

28 *Webster's New Compact Dictionary*, (Thompson Nelson Publishers, 1978), 243.

29 Museum of Antiquities. Online. 1997 http://museums.ncl.ac.uk/archive/arma/welc/beginner/page02.htm

30 Peter Thompson, M.Ed., *The Real Insider's Guide to Military Basic Training,* (Universal Publishers/uPUBLISH.com, 1998), 84.

31 Ibid, 91.

32 Walvoord & Zuck, *The Bible Knowledge Commentary, Old Testament,* (Cook Communications Ministries, 2000), 356

33 Ibid, 362

34 Ibid, 364

35 Ibid, 365

36 Oswald Chambers, *My Utmost for His Highest*, (Barbour Publishing, Inc.), July 8th devotional.

37 Henry H Halley, *Halley's Bible Handbook Revised Edition,* (Zondervan Publishing House, 1965), 415.

38 Merrill F Unger, *Concise Bible Dictionary*, (Tyndale House Publishers, Inc., 1974), 52.

39 Alfred J Kolatch, *The Jewish Book of Why,* (Jonathan David Publishers, Inc., 1995), 40-41.

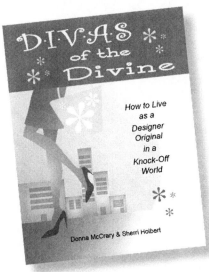

WALKING WITH GOD
WITH
Women's Conference

with
MINDY FERGUSON

To schedule Mindy Ferguson for a
Walking With God Women's Conference or as a guest speaker,
please visit www.fruitfulword.org

HENSLEY
PUBLISHING

CPSIA information can be obtained at www.ICGtesting.com
Printed in the USA
LVOW022347131211

259270LV00001B/6/P

9 781563 221057